How Smartphones Work

TITLES PUBLISHED BY SYMBIAN PRESS

- Wireless Java for Symbian Devices
  Jonathan Allin
  0471 486841   512pp   2001   Paperback
- Symbian OS Communications Programming
  Michael J Jipping
  0470 844302   418pp   2002   Paperback
- Programming for the Series 60 Platform and Symbian OS
  Digia
  0470 849487   550pp   2002   Paperback
- Symbian OS C++ for Mobile Phones, Volume 1
  Richard Harrison
  0470 856114   826pp   2003   Paperback
- Programming Java 2 Micro Edition on Symbian OS
  Martin de Jode
  0470 092238   498pp   2004   Paperback
- Symbian OS C++ for Mobile Phones, Volume 2
  Richard Harrison
  0470 871083   448pp   2004   Paperback
- Symbian OS Explained
  Jo Stichbury
  0470 021306   448pp   2004   Paperback
- Programming PC Connectivity Applications for Symbian OS
  Ian McDowall
  0470 090537   480pp   2004   Paperback
- Rapid Mobile Enterprise Development for Symbian OS
  Ewan Spence
  0470 014857   324pp   2005   Paperback
- Symbian for Software Leaders
  David Wood
  0470 016833   328pp   2005   Hardback
- Symbian OS Platform Security
  Craig Heath
  0470 018828   256pp   2006   Paperback
- How Smartphones Work
  Phil Northam
  0470 028866   228pp   2006   Hardback

How Smartphones Work

Symbian and the Mobile Phone Industry

Editor

Phil Northam

With

Freddie Gjertsen, Stephen Williams, John Forsyth, Bruce Carney, Simon Glassman, Mike Whittingham, Phil Spencer, Andrew Moran, Martin de Jode

Head of Symbian Press

Phil Northam

Managing Editors

Freddie Gjertsen
Satu McNabb

John Wiley & Sons, Ltd

Other Wiley Editorial Offices

John Wiley & Sons Inc., 111 River Street, Hoboken, NJ 07030, USA

Jossey-Bass, 989 Market Street, San Francisco, CA 94103-1741, USA

Wiley-VCH Verlag GmbH, Boschstr. 12, D-69469 Weinheim, Germany

John Wiley & Sons Australia Ltd, 42 McDougall Street, Milton, Queensland 4064, Australia

John Wiley & Sons (Asia) Pte Ltd, 2 Clementi Loop #02-01, Jin Xing Distripark, Singapore
129809

John Wiley & Sons Canada Ltd, 22 Worcester Road, Etobicoke, Ontario, Canada M9W 1L1

Wiley also publishes its books in a variety of electronic formats. Some content that appears
in print may not be available in electronic books.

ISBN-10 0-470-02886-6 (HB)

Typeset in 10/14pt Optima by Laserwords Private Limited, Chennai, India
Printed and bound by Graphos SA, Barcelona, Spain
This book is printed on acid-free paper responsibly manufactured from sustainable forestry
in which at least two trees are planted for each one used for paper production.

Contents

Contributors

Editor
Phil Northam
Head of Symbian Press

Chapter 1
Freddie Gjertsen
Managing Editor of Symbian Press

Chapter 2
From an original article by David Mery
Phil Northam
Head of Symbian Press

Chapter 3
Stephen Williams
Vice President of Finance and Operations, Symbian

Chapter 4
Phil Northam
Head of Symbian Press

Chapter 5
John Forsyth
Technical Account Director, Symbian

Chapter 6
Bruce Carney
Head of Developer Marketing and Services, Symbian

Chapter 7
Simon Glassman
Operator Account Director, Symbian

Chapter 8
Mike Whittingham
Product Portfolio Director, Hardware Adaptation, Symbian

Chapter 9
Phil Spencer
Manager of the Symbian Developer Community

Chapter 10
Andrew Moran
Head of Enterprise Market Development, Symbian

Chapter 11
Martin de Jode
Author of *Programming Java 2 Micro Edition on Symbian OS*

Symbian Press Editorial

Managing Editor
Freddie Gjertsen
Satu McNabb

Associate Editor
William Carnegie

Symbian Graphics and Photography/Cover design
James Mentz

Special thanks to
Richard Fitzgerald
Jason Parker

Acknowledgments

To everyone who contributed, many thanks, especially to Thomas and Freddie whose enthusiasm for the project has proven to be the motivation needed by a somewhat frazzled editor. Particular credit goes to the Symbian Press team (Freddie, William and the nefarious porpoises) who, as usual, stepped up to the plate when needed (if not before), and the LBC, the knights paladin of wit and banter.

Introduction

Thomas Chambers, Chief Financial Officer, Symbian

As I rush to leave my house to catch the train to work each morning I follow a ritual to see that I have everything I need. My checklist includes keys, money, credit cards, laptop (with accompanying power lead), iPod (these train journeys can be very dull!), train pass, any relevant documents, and, of course, my mobile phone. I hastily buy a newspaper on the way into the railway station to keep up to date with world news. Each morning I intend to have a productive journey into the office by preparing myself for the day ahead. Instead, my journey unfolds as it does on every other day. The train is full. There are no seats, there is nowhere to rest a laptop, no space to read my documents or the newspaper I have brought with me. I am left, as always, wondering why I have bothered to bring all this stuff. The only productive option on such a crowded train is to make a few phone calls and send some text messages with my one free hand, while clutching the train handrail with the other. At least my mobile phone has emails delivered to it (what did we do before email?). A cacophony of ring tones (sound bytes from the latest hit singles) tells me that everyone else is doing the same.

Not too long ago I would have been forced to wait until I arrived at the office to start my business day (or were the trains less crowded?). I was not an early adopter of mobile phones. I resisted the opportunity to stay permanently connected until I finally realized that not being permanently connected meant being permanently in the office. Mobile phones have allowed me to escape.

We are all becoming increasingly mobile. Or rather, we seek the freedom of being able to communicate with our friends, access our personal data, and still find information wherever we might be. Most mobile phones are able to offer users voice calls and small amounts of data transfer, such as text messages. Those that can offer significantly more than this are usually described as 'smartphones'. Smartphones now have the functionality of cameras, camcorders, video players, digital audio players, electronic organizers, portable radios and games consoles. They allow us access to technologies such as on-demand TV, over-the-air (OTA) email synchronization (in addition to push email), Internet access, WiFi access and electronic payment. Within a year of my writing this, the list will be longer and much more diverse.

The smartphone is today's key 'portable lifestyle support system'. We are seeing device convergence through addition of functionality to the mobile phone at a speed unprecedented in any other consumer or enterprise device. In 2004 there were in excess of 600 million mobile phones shipped, compared with 180 million laptop computers, 53 million digital cameras, 17 million digital TVs and seven million MP3 players. It is not surprising that the mobile phone is at the center of this convergence.

It is easy to forget that mobile phones have only been with us for a few years. In 1987, first-generation (1G) mobile phone technology was born as Nokia launched the Cityman NMT handportable (though not exactly portable by today's standards). In 1992 we were introduced to second-generation (2G) mobile phone technology and the first digital mobile phone networks. Today we have a range of third-generation (3G) mobile phones offering a rapidly expanding selection of services. Users can buy a smartphone targeted at their particular needs, with software and peripherals added to meet their personal requirements.

Despite the growing relevance of the mobile phone to our daily lives, very few words have been written to explain how the mobile phone industry really works, and fewer still on the smartphone industry. What are the major elements that come together to make it what it is, what is the infrastructure that surrounds it, and what are the choices available to the manufacturers and users of such devices? Perhaps this shortage of published information is due to the speed of technological advance, quickly causing books about mobile phones to become history books. Or perhaps it is because there are simply not enough people around who really do know what goes into a mobile phone.

I am constantly asked to explain how the parts of a mobile phone fit together in a way that puts everything in perspective without delving too deeply into complex technological detail. I am no engineer and in the past I too have struggled to explain some of the more complex aspects of the Symbian world to colleagues and friends. It is with this in mind that Symbian has put this book together. *How Smartphones Work* endeavors to give its readers a high-level understanding of what makes up a smartphone, the smartphone industry, and how it all comes together.

The amount of software embedded in mobile phones is expanding rapidly. In the past three years it has jumped from 2 MB to around 30 MB. Phone users can add additional software and content: data storage in mobile phones is set to expand rapidly in the coming years with the introduction of high-capacity memory cards, micro disk drives and other storage media. As mobile phones have assimilated increasing amounts of technology, it has become necessary for their resources to be managed in a way similar to those of a desktop computer. Symbian was created in 1998 by the world's leading mobile phone manufacturers to provide the industry-standard operating system for smartphones. That operating system is Symbian OS. Symbian OS is designed to maximize the potential of computing and communications in a constrained environment. It overcomes limitations in size, weight, battery life, screen size and memory while providing multitasking (the ability to complete several tasks simultaneously), a highly secure environment, communications compatibility between different mobile phones and differentiation in mobile phone design.

Symbian's business model is to take a royalty per unit on each mobile phone that contains Symbian OS – the company does not compete with other participants in the mobile phone value chain. Symbian's job is to understand new mobile phone technologies and to provide a framework that enables the industry to exploit them to their full potential. Symbian is creating its operating system not for what is required today, but for what will be required in the next few years. In this way it ensures that designers and manufacturers are able to develop new generations of mobile phones. The company cooperates with other players in the mobile phone industry to determine and drive the future of mobile phone design and evolution. Symbian works with mobile phone manufacturers, silicon providers, network operators, consumer and enterprise application developers and programmers to optimize the performance of mobile phones and the features available on them.

At Symbian, I am in the unique position of being able to gather together a group of industry experts to explain the key elements of the evolving 'smartphone' category. Every chapter of this book is written with a unique insight into the evolution of the industry. You do not need to read this book from cover to cover. I recommend that you review all of the content and then delve into the specific areas where you feel that you would like to know more.

We will continue to see significant developments in features, performance, memory capacity and computing power in mobile phones in the coming years. In 1965 George Moore, cofounder of Intel, devised Moore's Law which he stated as 'data density on integrated circuits will double every 18 months' – this is expected to hold true for at least another two decades. I believe that the smartphone will become increasingly akin to a server in your pocket, constantly in touch with the outside world via network operators offering the user access on the move to a range of services and data.

What does this mean for my 'portable lifestyle support system' and my last-minute lifestyle? Both are in for a revolution. Assuming that I am still rushing to leave my house each morning to catch a train to work, all that I will need to remember is my smartphone. The door will be locked using Bluetooth as I leave my house. Money and credit cards will be history since my mobile phone will contain a retina scanner and fingerprint reader which can authorize any payment (no matter how small) to my mobile phone account (including my train fare, which is rarely small). I will be able to instantly download and store information for the day's meeting or the latest news onto my smartphone, which will also store my entire music collection. It's a shame that the train will still be full.

If you too are excited by the rapid device and technology convergence around smartphones, then this book will give you an understanding of what makes it all happen. Inevitably, it will become outdated as technology and the industry advance beyond our current understanding, but since Symbian is designing its operating system for tomorrow's mobile phones, I hope that this book will at least put you at the forefront of mobile phone evolution today.

How Smartphones Work

On June 24 1998, a new company, Symbian, was formed. It marked the coming together of the world's largest mobile phone manufacturers at that time – Ericsson, Motorola and Nokia – with a leading-edge software company, Psion. Their vision was simple: in the future, mobile phones were going to be used for more than just phone calls – they were going to transmit and manage data. In short, they would have the ability to be the 'remote controls' that we would use to manage our lives, in the same way that the personal computer provided us the means to manage business from the desktop. To realize this vision, they would need a powerful standards-based software platform, and Symbian would be the company to develop it.

How Smartphones Work is a look at the new industry that has sprung up around smartphone technology. Anyone familiar with the mobile phone industry will be aware of the tremendous pace of development and innovation, and how the introduction of the smartphone has entwined the futures of the mobile phone and software industries. Together these industries are proving that they have the ability to bring new innovations to mobile phone technology, building better phones faster and more cheaply, creating completely new products, and totally redefining the way we communicate.

Part I of this book is an introduction to the smartphone environment, or you might say, 'what makes Symbian OS work'. It begins by examining the principles of mobile telephony, the way a mobile phone network works and evolution to third-generation (3G) technology. We will explain why an advanced operating system is required for smartphones, and why the unusual constraints of the mobile phone environment mean that there have to be engineering compromises when creating a mobile telephony product. We will also discover how these unique demands in the mobile phone environment have brought the industry together to create Symbian OS. Symbian OS is owned by the mobile phone industry for the mobile phone industry, and it creates a common, open, standard operating system for mobile phones.

One of the central themes of this book is understanding the nature of 'openness'. The future of smartphones depends on the ability of a large number of companies to bring value and innovation to smartphones, either during their creation or when they are in the hands of a customer. In Part II, we look at what makes smartphones work – the ecosystem of innovation around Symbian and Symbian OS.

CHAPTER 1

The Basics of a Mobile Phone System

There are currently six billion people on this planet and nearly two billion of them use mobile phones. However, the majority of mobile phone users have only the vaguest notion of how their mobile phone actually functions and of the technology on which it is based. This chapter provides an overview of the workings of a mobile phone and the infrastructure that is necessary for mobility.

The primary function of a telephone of any kind is, of course, to allow you to talk to someone who is beyond shouting distance. A standard telephone allows long distance conversation by converting the sound waves of your voice into electrical signals. Mobile telephony is based on the same principle but, lacking connecting cables, a mobile phone instead converts the sound waves of your voice into radio waves which it transmits through the air; a mobile phone receiving a call converts radio waves into sound waves. This is the essence of a mobile phone: it is a battery-powered radio transceiver.

Precious spectrum

The signals that a mobile phone emits are not transmitted directly to other mobile phones, but to fixed transceivers (base stations) in the locality of the mobile phone making the call. These fixed transceivers then transfer the call into the existing cable-based telephone network, which in turn relays the signals to a standard telephone or to another mobile phone (via a radio transceiver local to the mobile phone being called).

Mobile phones use frequencies within the radio band of the electromagnetic spectrum to transmit and receive calls. The electromagnetic spectrum is a limited natural resource, with the radio frequency band comprising a subset of frequencies within it. This subset is used for a range of purposes (for example, radio and TV broadcasting, emergency communication and navigation aids) and, consequently, the number of frequencies available for mobile phone calls is limited. This entails that the number of mobile phone calls being transmitted within a given area is also limited.

Radio frequency band

Mobile phones and their base stations transmit and receive signals using electromagnetic waves or 'radio signals'. Electromagnetic radiation consists of oscillating electric and magnetic fields and the frequency, the number of times per second at which the wave oscillates, determines their properties and the use that can be made of them. Frequencies are measured in Hertz (Hz), where 1 Hz is one oscillation per second, 1 kHz is a thousand oscillations per second, 1 MHz a million, and 1 GHz a thousand million oscillations per second. Frequencies between 30 kHz and 300 GHz are widely used for telecommunications, including broadcast radio and television, and comprise the 'radio frequency (RF) band'.

The cellular solution

Base stations act as the gateway for mobile phones into the cable-based or 'fixed' telephone network. It was originally assumed that a single, powerful radio transceiver could provide radio coverage for mobile phones across a large geographic area. However, due to the limited amount of available electromagnetic spectrum, this model meant that only a small number of people would be able to use mobile phones – basically those prepared to pay the premium for access to this small number of available frequencies.

However, an answer to the problem of limited frequency availability was developed shortly after the Second World War. The solution was to use a grid of low-power fixed transceivers that, because of their low power, would communicate only within a limited geographic area (a cell). The beauty of this system (or cellular network) is that it allows frequencies to be re-used from cell to cell, thereby maximizing the traffic that a limited number of frequencies can carry.

Base station

A base station is a fixed transceiver that acts as the link between a mobile phone and the landline network. Mobile phone networks are composed of an array of base stations that in combination provide coverage for a network. Each base station's range of reception is determined by the area it covers and the number of calls that it is likely to process.

In remote areas, base stations are likely to provide less power than those in densely populated areas but they cover a larger area of transmission (their coverage is more thinly spread). Buildings and terrain limit range, so a city will need many base stations to handle both this and the large number of people using the network. If you look at maps of the areas covered by mobile phone networks, you will find that the pattern of network base stations follows population density, covering main roads and population centers first.

Single transceiver for area   Cellular network

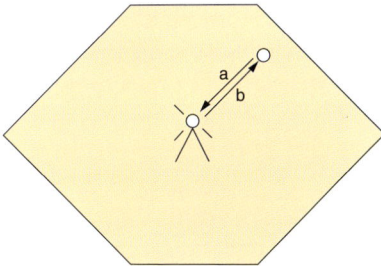

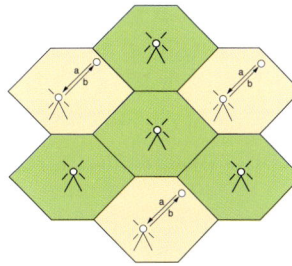

Within the same geographic area, a single transceiver allows frequencies a and b to be used only once; with a cellular network they can be used for three separate conversations

Fitting cells together

In theory, an ideal cellular network is a group of hexagonal cells evenly spread out across a geographic area. This is possible in practice, but only in a perfectly flat area without buildings or other objects to block the radio waves. Though lower frequencies tend to penetrate through obstacles well, higher frequencies tend to be stopped by objects in their path. For example, a plasterboard wall will completely stop light, but will have almost no noticeable effect on radio waves. More absorbent materials within buildings will, however, stop radio waves.

As human populations rarely live in areas that are entirely flat and free from obstacles, cell coverage varies considerably according to the terrain, the location of a cell's antenna, intervening buildings, landmarks and other barriers.

As a rule, base stations are adapted to their surroundings. In rural, sparsely populated areas a base station is likely to cover a wider geographic area with a weaker signal, whereas in a city center it will cover a smaller geographic area with a stronger signal. A greater number of smaller cells allows greater capacity in areas where there are likely to be more users of the network.

Moving from cell to cell
The use of multiple cells in a mobile phone network means that, as a mobile phone moves from place to place with its owner, it will also move from cell to cell. The mechanism for handling this differs depending on the type of network and the circumstances of the change in position. The general rule is that as you move toward the edge of a cell, that cell's base station notes that your signal strength is diminishing. Meanwhile, the base station in the cell that you are moving toward (which is listening and measuring signal strength on all frequencies, not just its own) observes that a phone's signal strength is increasing. During this process, your phone gets a signal on a control channel telling it to change frequencies and, thus, your mobile phone is switched to the new cell. This process is known as 'handover'.

Summary
Mobile phones are mobile because they are radio transceivers that use the electromagnetic spectrum to transmit voice and data. In order to maximize the use of the available spectrum, cellular networks are used. An added advantage of such networks is that mobile phones need not transmit signals over vast distances and therefore require less power and can have smaller batteries (which is vital for a phone to be truly mobile).

From analog to 4G

A key element in the proliferation of more practical, useful mobile phones was – and is – the use of standards. Far from trivial to implement, and often difficult to agree upon, international industry standards for mobile phone technologies are vital to the uptake of the technology. Standards encourage competition by making technologies open to newcomers, and they also make those technologies universal. At the simplest level it means that the same phone and network technology can be used in, for example, both Denmark and Italy, allowing for economies of scale in manufacturing.

Standards

It would be easy to enter into a philosophical debate about what defines a 'standard' – if customers adopt a technology, whether or not it is 'approved' by a standards body, it can become the technology standard in use. If a manufacturer creates a product or innovation with a technology that is not included in approved standards, it is called a 'proprietary technology'.

For the purposes of this book, when we use 'standard' we mean the properties that a product or service should have, as agreed upon within the mobile phone industry by mobile phone standards bodies. For instance, the Bluetooth SIG defines the standards for Bluetooth technology. Once a common standard is defined and made public it becomes possible for competing manufacturers to adhere to it and so ensure interoperability of services. For instance, at the most basic level, phones made by company X and company Y will both work on the network operated by network operator A.

More details of the standards supported by Symbian OS are available in Chapter 2.

1G: Analog mobile telephony

First-generation (1G) mobile phones were analog devices that originated (because of their power requirements) as in-car phones. These phones laid the foundations for later, more successful mobile networks, though they were flawed in many ways.

One of the most successful introductions of an analog cellular network was in Scandinavia. The NMT standard was agreed upon and adopted by Sweden, Denmark, Norway and Finland, ensuring that users could communicate seamlessly between and within these countries using the same system. This venture illustrated the feasibility of a transnational cellular phone system.

Elsewhere in Europe, major national telecommunications monopolies decided to develop their own cellular systems. Thus, in 1991 the European landscape was a patchwork of national systems employing incompatible standards designed to satisfy national interests. But while the impossibility of roaming across Europe was bad enough, this was not the only problem with the analog networks.

The UK cellular network

In 1982, the UK government announced that two analog cellular licenses would be made available. These licenses were purchased by two consortia: Cellnet (a government-backed alliance between British Telecom and Securicor) and Vodafone (including Racal, Millicom and other partners).

A UK government committee decided which analog standard would be adopted. It rejected the Scandinavian NMT standard as incapable of delivering sufficient capacity to central London and other standards were seen as proprietary or unproven. In the end it was decided to copy the USA's AMPS standard, which (after some adjustment) was renamed the total access communications system (TACS).

What this process illustrates is the vacuum in which analog standards were selected. Compatibility was precluded when governments set about reviewing available standards and selecting and honing those which they believed to be best suited to their nation.

Analog networks also had an intrinsic flaw – they were inefficient. Only one conversation could be carried out on a given frequency. Or, to be more exact, a given channel. A radio channel is a pair of frequencies, one used to transmit and one to receive. The advantage of using a channel over using a single frequency is that it allows a user to talk and to listen at the same time, rather than talking and then listening in turn, as with a walkie-talkie.

This inefficiency severely restricted the number of people who could use a network, with the result that the cost per user was high. If mobile phones were to appeal to a mass market, analog was not up to the job. Going digital

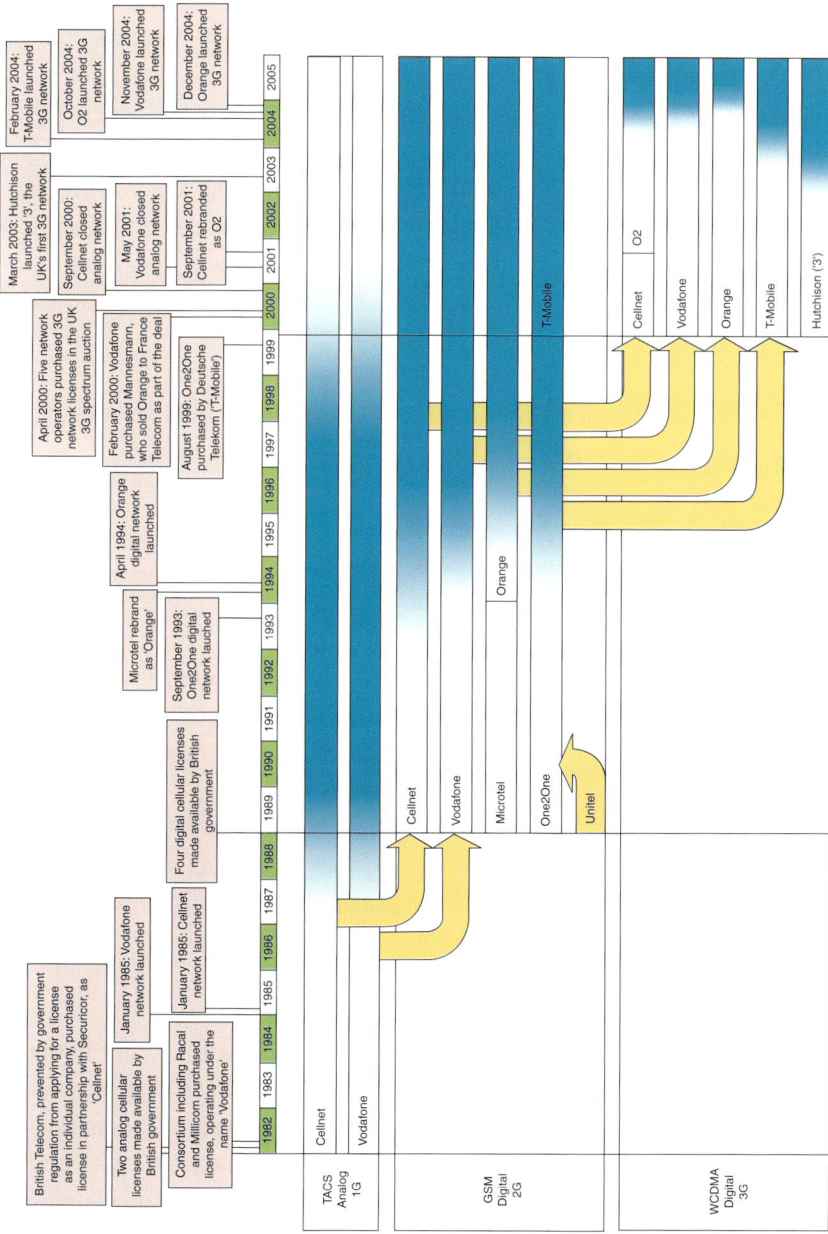

The development of mobile phone standards within the UK

was seen as the best way to overcome the problems, handle the anticipated surge in users, and incorporate the transmission of data (such as text messages).

2G: Digital mobile telephony

A digital system allows a greater volume of calls over a given frequency than an analog system. Analog systems transmit voice messages as sound waves. When you speak into an analog mobile phone, your voice wave is linked to a radio wave and transmitted. In digital systems, voice messages are transmitted as a stream of zeroes and ones. When you speak into a digital mobile phone, your voice wave is converted into a binary pattern before being transmitted.

Mobile phone systems all utilize some method to allow multiple users to share the system concurrently. The three methods for doing this are:

- FDM: Frequency Division Multiplexing
- TDMA: Time Division Multiple Access
- CDMA: Code Division Multiple Access

Analog mobile phone systems utilize FDM. The FDM system divides the available frequency into channels. Each conversation is given a channel. When the system runs out of channels in a given area, no more telephone calls can be connected.

Digital mobile phone systems utilize the radio spectrum more efficiently and allow multiple users to share the same physical channel. This allows more than one person to hold a conversation on the same frequency, without causing interference.

There are two principal competing digital technologies, which differ in the way they utilize the spectrum: TDMA and CDMA. In a TDMA system, your encoded voice is digitized and then placed on a radio frequency channel with other calls. TDMA chops the channel into sequential time slices and each user takes turns transmitting and receiving. One call uses the channel at any given moment, but only for a short burst. The channel is then momentarily surrendered to other calls to allow them their 'short burst' of air time.

In a CDMA system, your encoded voice is digitized and divided into packets. These packets are tagged with 'codes'. All calls are transmitted simultaneously and the packets mix with all of the other packets of traffic in the local CDMA network as they are routed towards their destination. The receiving system only accepts the packets with the codes destined for it.

As these concepts are difficult to envisage, the following analogy may make this clearer. Imagine a room full of people, all trying to hold conversations in pairs. With TDMA, each couple takes a turn to talk. They keep their turns short by only saying one sentence at a time. As there is never more than one person speaking in the room at any given moment, no one has to worry about being heard over the background din. With CDMA, all the couples talk at the same time, but each uses a different language. Because none of the other listeners understand any language other than that of the individual to whom they are listening, the background din doesn't cause any major interference and the conversation can continue.

FDM systems typically allow one call per 10 KHz or 30 KHz of spectrum. Early TDMA systems tripled the capacity of FDM systems, and subsequent advances in TDMA should provide 40 times the carrying capacity of FDM systems. CDMA further improves on the efficiency, and so capacity, of TDMA. There are no exact figures for the capacity of CDMA systems: it is always possible to add one more caller to a CDMA channel. However, once a certain point is passed, a channel becomes polluted and it becomes difficult to retrieve an error-free data stream for any of the participants.

Digital standards

The introduction of digital systems allowed mobile networks to transmit data in addition to voice. It also presented an opportunity to standardize the incompatible, and therefore not interoperable, analog standards used in different European countries. Incompatible national standards did not make long-term economic sense. Given the daunting research and development costs facing operators and manufacturers, it was essential to be able to exploit the economies of scale inherent in global market penetration. Domestic market revenues simply wouldn't justify sustained programs of investment. At a minimum, a Europe-wide market was necessary.

The Groupe Spéciale Mobile (GSM) was formed, comprising the telecommunications associations of 26 European countries. Its objective was to develop the specification for a pan-European mobile communications network, capable of supporting the many millions of subscribers expected to use mobile communications in the years ahead.

It is unlikely that this standard would have proliferated but for the political backing it received. The then European Economic Community was seeking ways to further integrate European nations and this was clearly one. Under various monikers, European governance has proved especially successful in undertaking highly bureaucratic and technical projects (from the recommended degree of curvature in a banana to the specifications of manufactured goods) and creating 'European' standards. A unifying standard for digital cellular services would clearly serve the aims of European politicians eager to create a single market within Europe – easing the burden of traveling and trading amongst the member states of the EEC. A 1986 meeting of the European Council (the European Heads of State) lead to a directive supporting the introduction of GSM services. The directive ensured that every member state would reserve the 900 MHz frequency blocks for the introduction of digital telephony.

GSM

Groupe Spéciale Mobile was the original meaning of the acronym 'GSM' – the organization that defined the GSM standard. The group which sets the standards is now known as the 'GSA', or GSM Association and 'GSM' has come to mean global system for mobile communications.

GSM is the most widely used digital mobile phone system and is the wireless telephone standard in Europe. Defined as a pan-European open standard for a digital cellular telephone network to support voice, data, text messaging and cross-border roaming, it is now one of the world's main 2G/2.5G digital wireless standards.

GSM differs from first-generation wireless systems in that it uses digital technology and time-division multiple access (TDMA) transmission methods.

2.5G

While the terms '2G' and '3G' are officially defined, '2.5G' is not. 'Two-point-five G' is used to describe 2G systems that have implemented packet-switched transmission in addition to circuit-switched.

Packet switching and circuit switching

Packet switching is a technique whereby information (voice or data) is broken up into packets, of a few KB each, prior to being transmitted. The network then processes the packets, routing them between different destinations based on addressing data within each packet. This method optimizes use of network resources, as the resources are needed only during the handling of each packet. This is an ideal model for irregular data communication, and works well also for voice, video and other streamed data. Mobile phones with packet-switched communication appear to be 'always connected' to the data network, whereas in the case of circuit-switched connections, it takes around 30 seconds to connect from a mobile phone to an ISP. Most traffic over the Internet uses packet switching and the Internet is basically a connectionless network. Voice calls using the Internet's packet-switched system are possible. Each end of the conversation is broken down into packets that are reassembled at the other end.

The predecessor to packet switching was circuit switching. Circuit-switched networks, for instance the cable-based voice telephone network, set up a communication circuit for a call which is dedicated to the participants in that call. For the duration of the connection, all resources on that circuit are unavailable for other users. Accordingly, circuit-switched connections are charged by duration (unlike packet-switched connections, which are charged by volume of data transferred).

2.5G provides some of the benefits of 3G (such as packet switching) and can use the existing 2G infrastructure of GSM and CDMA networks. The transmission method synonymous with 2.5G is GPRS – other standards, such as EDGE for GSM and CDMA2000 1x-RTT for CDMA, officially qualify as 3G services (because they have a data rate of above 144 kbit/s), but are also considered by most to be 2.5G services because they are slower than 'true' or high-bandwidth 3G services.

The major advantage that 2.5G offers is 'always-on' capability. Being packet-based, 2.5G technologies allow for the use of infrastructure and facilities only when a transaction is required, rather than requiring dedicated channels for the duration of a connection. This allows the infrastructure to be used more efficiently and service delivery to be improved.

Using GPRS as a bearer for wireless access protocol (WAP), for instance, allows for the use of WAP on a per-transaction rather than a per-minute-of-use basis. More important, perhaps, is the ability for GPRS to automate services through its always-on capability. For example, a GPRS customer can receive content or services without manually invoking a service or trans-action. This has significant advantages for implementing mobile commerce and location-based services.

WAP

Wireless application protocol is a set of communication protocol standards that make it possible to access online services from a mobile phone. WAP was conceived by four companies: Ericsson, Motorola, Nokia, and Unwired Planet. This technology helped mobile phone manufacturers make the leap to Internet connectivity, albeit in a basic manner. Unfortunately, WAP raised industry expectations way beyond what it could deliver. Costly – and probably misplaced – advertising campaigns practically promised virtual reality, whereas the protocol was designed for basic Internet connectivity, for instance allowing users to pick up their email through a simple interface.

Many regard WAP as a 'dead' technology, but it remains an extremely important part of the mobile user experience: in Japan, it is the basis of Sha-Mail, a rival to NTT DoCoMo's i-mode. It is also hugely successful in Korea. In Europe, WAP has taken its rightful place as an enabling technology, rather than a brand in its own right, and is used by Vodafone Live! and T-Mobile's T-Zones.

The WAP Forum is an industry association with over 200 members and is now part of the Open Mobile Association.

3G

The principle benefit of 3G networks is that rapid data transfer speeds are possible, making it practical to transmit large amounts of data to a mobile phone. This introduces the capacity for phone users to browse the Internet and to download music and videos.

In 2006, 3G phones and services are starting to proliferate across Europe. Governments auctioned the licenses to run these services from 1999 onwards, with the resultant fierce bidding wars driving the license prices to exorbitant levels – in the UK the government raised £22.5 billion selling 3G licenses. It would seem that these high costs caused a delay in the roll-out of 3G services in these countries. The first country which introduced 3G on a large commercial scale was Japan. In 2005, about 40% of subscribers used 3G networks only and 2G was on the way out in Japan. It is expected that during 2006 the transition from 2G to 3G will be largely completed.

Another benefit that the move from 2G to 3G appeared to offer was an opportunity to standardize mobile phone standards and so create a single, worldwide radio transmission standard. The process of unifying the numerous international standards has proved to be extremely difficult. A 3G standard called IMT-2000 did emerge, but this standardized not on a technology but rather on a set of requirements (2 Mbit/s maximum data rate indoors, 384 kbit/s outdoors). It therefore represents several standards under one banner rather than a single standard. The major standards are listed below.

- W-CDMA was developed by NTT DoCoMo for FOMA, its 3G network. Later NTT DoCoMo submitted the specification to the International Telecommunication Union (ITU) as a candidate for the international 3G standard known as IMT-2000. The ITU eventually accepted W-CDMA as part of the IMT-2000 family of 3G standards. Later, W-CDMA was selected as the technology for UMTS, the 3G successor to GSM. Despite the similarity in name, W-CDMA has very little to do with CDMA (see below). In the mobile phone world, the term CDMA can refer to either the Code Division Multiple Access spread spectrum multiplexing technique, or to the CDMA family of standards developed by Qualcomm, including cdmaOne (or IS-95) and CDMA2000 (or IS-2000).
- CDMA2000 is a 3G mobile telecommunications standard that uses CDMA, a multiple access scheme for digital radio, to send voice, data and signaling

data (such as a dialed telephone number) between mobile phones and cell sites. CDMA-2000 is one of the approved radio interfaces for the IMT-2000 standard and a successor to 2G CDMA (IS-95, branded cdmaOne).

- TD-SCDMA (Time Division Synchronous Code Division Multiple Access) is a 3G mobile telecommunications standard being developed by the Chinese Academy of Telecommunications Technology (CATT), Datang and Siemens AG, in an attempt to develop Chinese technology. It is based on spread-spectrum CDMA technology.

4G

Logically enough (or not, as we may discover), the next step beyond 3G will be 4G. There are already rumblings of the introduction of 4G networks in Japan, with NTT DoCoMo announcing that they plan to introduce 4G services from 2006, four years earlier than anticipated. This early move may allow them to establish a global standard for 4G technology.

Inside a mobile phone

Individual smartphones contain a mass of highly complex and rigorously developed technology. The components within a mobile phone must be able to transmit and receive radio waves, regulate the power of the phone and the usage of the battery, and, in the case of smartphones, operate as a telephone and as a computer.

An internal inspection of a mobile phone yields little information about its workings, presenting few easily recognizable components. The principle item protected by a mobile phone's plastic casing is a circuit board in which a range of chips are embedded. To an inexpert eye it is very difficult to distinguish anything from this mass of circuitry, and it is certainly impossible to determine how any of it allows a mobile phone call to be made, or for that same phone to support a rich user interface on which applications may be run.

Inside the Symbian OS-based smartphone illustrated (a Sony Ericsson P900), you will see that the circuit board is divided into discrete areas by insulating metal borders. These divisions, and the metal casing which is placed over the circuit board, prevent the different sub-systems from disrupting one another (all of the various components generate radio noise due to the frequencies at which they operate). As this implies, each sub-system performs a different role within the phone.

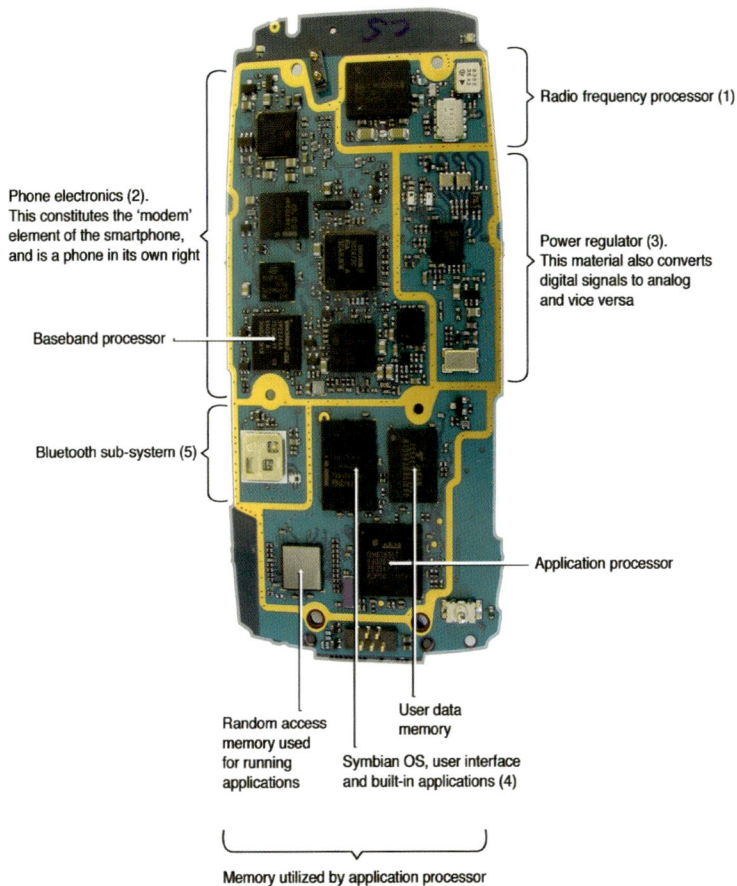

Radio frequency processor (1)

Phone electronics (2).
This constitutes the 'modem'
element of the smartphone,
and is a phone in its own right

Power regulator (3).
This material also converts
digital signals to analog
and vice versa

Baseband processor

Bluetooth sub-system (5)

Application processor

Random access
memory used
for running
applications

User data
memory

Symbian OS, user interface
and built-in applications (4)

Memory utilized by application processor

The circuitry of a Sony Ericsson P900 smartphone

The sub-systems take the following roles: 1) radio frequency processor, 2) phone electronics, 3) power regulation, 4) Symbian OS components, and 5) Bluetooth.

The radio frequency processor, in the top right-hand corner of the circuit board, amplifies power to the appropriate frequency for transmission and communicates with the phone's antenna. In essence, it sends and receives the radio signals necessary for mobile phone calls.

The phone electronics element of the circuit board, below and to the left of the radio frequency processor contains the modem and supporting

5) The Bluetooth sub-system

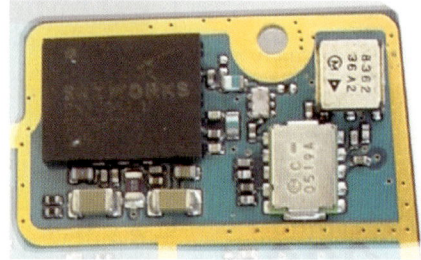

1) The radio frequency processor components

electronics which control the making and receiving of phone calls. The baseband processor is part of this collection. More information about this and the application processor can be found in Chapter 8.

4) The 'Symbian OS components' of the circuit board (more details in Chapter 8)

2) The 'phone components' of the circuit board

The bottom half of the circuit board constitutes the element of the phone specific to Symbian OS. This could be characterized as a computer bolted on to a phone (the 'phone' being all the circuitry above it). The chips that are visible are the application processor and the various memory units that it utilizes. These units of memory have different functions: one stores code for Symbian OS and its user interface (ROM), another is used for running applications (RAM), and a third for storing user data (user data memory). Further detail on the different memory types can be found in Chapter 4.

The remaining interesting section contains the power regulating components of the phone. These take power from the phone's battery and distribute it through the system as appropriate. This set of components is also responsible for converting digital signals to analog, and vice versa. This is especially relevant to mobile phones, which transmit voice and data digitally but, of

Clockwise from top left: A camera, an LCD, a memory card, and a vibrator

course, use microphones and speakers to transmit the human voice, which is analog, to the phone's user.

Some of the peripherals which are controlled and regulated by the circuitry on the circuit board, are the camera, the LCD, the vibrator and a memory card which can be used to store additional data – for instance as an extension of a phone's memory for user data, or to contain a full-length movie.

CHAPTER 2

Why a Different Operating System Is Needed

The term 'operating system' is one most people are familiar with but, for the most part, give little thought to. This is usually because an operating system tends to be rather unobtrusive. If you are familiar with the concept of an operating system you are likely to point to the desktop PC, but operating systems – of varying degrees of complexity – are embedded in all kinds of electronic devices. Simply put, the operating system is just a term for the software that makes your device (be that a computer, a smartphone, a DVD player or a television, to name just a few) function when you interact with it. The operating system is the brain of an electronic device, enabling communication with all its different parts and making them work together as intended.

Operating system

An operating system (OS) is historically the minimum set of software needed to manage a device's hardware and apportion it to application programs. In practice, 'OS' is now used to mean all software including the kernel, device drivers, communications, graphics, data management, user interface (UI) framework, system shell application, and utility applications.

Symbian OS was designed with the specific constraints of handheld computing in mind. As a result, the operating system is optimized to run efficiently on devices which have limited resources and battery power (in contrast to operating systems designed for desktop PCs, which can rely upon having a constant supply of mains power and vast quantities of RAM and hard disk available).

But if all these products have the need for an operating system, why do they not use the same one? The simple answer is that the devices are different: different types of hardware work in unique ways and need to be communicated with in different ways by software. For example, imagine going on a tour of London with the best tour guide London has to offer. You would expect to learn a lot. But if you were touring Tokyo the following week, you would not reasonably expect that same guide to be able to join you and give you an experience of comparable quality.

Similarly, the design of a particular operating system may suit one use, but not another. A desktop PC has a vast amount of storage space and a large amount of memory in which to run programs. It also benefits from an effectively limitless power supply. The operating system for your PC can therefore be allowed to occupy many gigabytes of storage space and several megabytes of execution memory. This is not true of a smartphone. Using our friendly tour guide as an example once more, if you are in London for a 12-hour stopover, but he specializes in two-day tours, his services are inappropriate for your needs.

In this chapter, we look at the unique demands of the environment that shapes the mobile phone, and what kind of operating system is needed to create best-in-class smartphones.

Smartphone

Symbian defines a smartphone as a mobile phone using an operating system based on industry standards, designed for the requirements of advanced mobile telephony communication on 2.5G and 3G networks. This combination of a powerful software platform with mobile telephony enables the introduction of advanced data services and innovation both by device creators and a wider industry of software developers.

This contrasts with the concept of a 'feature phone' (see Chapter 5), which is a customized version of a mobile phone (for instance, it might include a music player). Unlike a smartphone, a feature phone does not allow for more than basic personalization by the user (in other words, new applications exploiting the functionality of the phone's operating system cannot be added).

Voice plus

While it may sound obvious, the primary requirement of the mobile phone market is that all products are great for making phone calls. The smartphone market extends from voice-centric phones with information capability (such as S60 phones and DoCoMo's FOMA phones) to information-centric devices with voice capability (such as UIQ and Series 80 phones). (For more information about these user interfaces, please refer to Chapter 6.) Smartphones integrate the features and capabilities of a personal digital assistant (PDA) with the abilities of a traditional mobile phone in a single unit.

The mobile environment is unique, and any mobile device has different requirements from those of devices such as PCs or fixed domestic appliances. Scaling down a desktop PC operating system or bolting communication capabilities onto a small, basic operating system would result in fundamental compromises. The conclusion is that an operating system is needed that is designed specifically to meet the key characteristics of the mobile environment, namely:

- Mobile phones are both small and mobile.
- Mobile phones address a mass market which includes a huge variety of consumer segments, such as enterprise and professional users.
- Mobile phone manufacturers need to differentiate their products in order to innovate and compete in a fast-evolving market.

An appropriate operating system has to enable independent technology and software vendors to develop software and services.

The only way to expand the mobile phone market is to create good products – and the only way to create good products is to address each of these characteristics and ensure that technology does not limit functionality.

Designs on a mass market

Product reliability is a major issue for mobile phone manufacturers. If data is lost in a personal mobile phone, it causes a loss of trust between the user and the manufacturer's brand; a mobile phone must therefore be at least as resilient as a paper diary or agenda. From a commercial point of view, recalling mobile phones deployed in their tens of thousands to install updates is a last resort – so a mobile phone should never lock up or come with a major software defect. Moreover, mobile phones are often not turned off for long periods at a time, and therefore memory cannot be recovered in this way. To use a term we are all familiar with, it should never need a 'reboot', which is in contrast to desktop computers where bugs, crashes and reboots are not unexpected.

A robust and reliable operating system is perfectly achievable, and even though no one can guarantee bug-free software, a good operating system makes it much easier to write robust and reliable software. Reliability depends on good software engineering and a good error-handling framework. Engineering best practice greatly helps to reduce the number and severity of bugs, while the error-handling framework enables graceful recovery from errors such as running out of memory, low battery power or dropping a communication link.

In contrast to a desktop PC, a mobile phone will contain megabytes of memory as opposed to gigabytes, and this means that its operating system needs to keep an accurate track of limited memory resources to ensure peak performance all times. Applications and system modules that allocate memory need to cater for the possibility that it might not be available and to ensure that the user experience is minimally disrupted, even if this does occur.

However, reliability alone is not enough to make a good product. Sound consumer design is also necessary for:

- applications that take advantage of the mobile phone's unique characteristics as well as its environment
- products to meet current usability standards and future developments in wireless technology
- ease of use – if a feature is too complex to use, then it cannot justify either the time it took to develop or the space it takes in the device.

An operating system targeted at mobile phones must support these design principles by offering a high-level of integration of communications and personal information such as agenda, calendar and contacts.

Reliable connections

Accessing remote data, sending email, synchronizing calendars – all these require some type of connection. The very fact that you're mobile means that a wireless connection is going to be preferable – whether using the mobile phone network or using built-in connectivity such as infrared, Bluetooth or WiFi.

Even today, wireless connectivity is patchy and wide-area wireless networks are – and always will be – slower than wired networks. Different network standards around the world further limit connectivity, and occasional fade-outs while moving, together with incomplete coverage, especially in remote areas, buildings or while airborne, add to the likelihood of a dropped connection. It would be unwise for a mobile phone's operating system to be designed to rely on a permanent mobile connection as it is very frustrating for the user – perhaps part way through downloading an email – when it is dropped.

An operating system must take this into account by allowing its users to manipulate their personal information even when no connection is available. In short, the mobile phone must have built-in processing power, and it is up to the operating system to support this. It must also ensure a smooth transition between being a 'window' on the network and a self-sufficient device.

This occasionally connected environment requires an operating system with genuine multitasking, communications-capable real-time performance and a rich suite of communications protocols. In addition to the real-time requirement to maintain connections, the operating system must provide mechanisms to handle dropped connections gracefully and inform the user in an appropriate way. To provide a smooth transition to the user and to be

API

Historically, API has stood for 'application programming interface'. In practice, an API is any interface that enables one program to use facilities provided by another, whether calling that program, or being called by it. At a higher level, an API is a set of functionality delivered by an operating system, and the mix of APIs in that particular system tells you what that system can do. To put it another way, an API is the 'hook' by which a software developer links an application to the functionality that they wish to use in an operating system.

able to support network standards (such as the transition from 2.5G to 3G), the operating system has to provide a rich set of application programming interfaces (APIs) to ensure that applications can fully benefit from current connectivity possibilities and also take advantage of new protocols as they are implemented.

Product diversity

Advanced mobile phones, or smartphones, come in all shapes – from traditional designs resembling today's mobile phones with main input via the phone keypad, to 'tablet' designs operated with a stylus, to phones with large screens and small keyboards, as the figure shows.

Different styles of smartphone

The different input mechanisms and form factors strongly influence the intended primary use of the device in question. With a very small screen and no more than a keypad, the main use tends to be voice calls. With pen input, browsing is quite convenient, but data entry is less so. A keyboard is obviously the most practical mechanism for entering a large amount of data. These distinctions imply that user interfaces are ultimately both device- and market-dependent.

Product differentiation is not just a matter of operating system design. An operating-system vendor must allow its licensees the freedom to innovate and develop new product lines. The decision as to whether or not to allow this is a key feature of a vendor's commercial model.

To support distinct phone families and yet maximize code reuse, Symbian focuses on the common code, Symbian OS; this includes a multitasking multithreaded core, a user interface framework, data services enablers, application engines and integrated personal information management (PIM) functionality and wireless communications. Phone manufacturers are active participants in software development, creating a large development organization to extend Symbian OS. This results in developers among licensees and partners having access to source code and ensuring that Symbian OS remains an 'open standard' – open and advanced.

Open platform

An operating system for the mass market must be open to innovation by independent software vendors, enterprise IT departments, network operators and mobile phone manufacturers. Even though mobile phones are small and mobile, they offer facilities as rich as those found on desktop computers, in addition to basic functions such as voice and data communication. The operating system has to support both conventional and mobile computing conventions, and developers need knowledge of both. This implies a manageable learning curve, standard development languages such as C++ and Java, along with software development kits (SDKs), tools, documentation, books, technical support and training.

To reduce the time to market, developers should become proficient in as short a time as possible. It is necessary to support standards that they may already know or can easily learn from a multitude of sources. Such standards also make the platform more open and hence more attractive to developers.

Traditional standards such as Unicode for internationalization, a POSIX API (POSIX is the collective name used to describe the family of related standards which define the application program interface, API, for software), and Java are a must, but for an operating system to take its place in the connected world, open standards such as TCP/IP, POP3, IMAP4, SMTP,

SMS, MMS, Bluetooth, OBEX (OBject EXchange, a communications proto-col that facilitates the exchange of data between devices), WAP, i-mode, and SyncML must also be supported (these terms are explained in the list of supported standards, below).

SMS

The Short Message Service (SMS) is available on digital mobile phone networks and allows text messages of up to 160 characters to be sent and received by a mobile phone via a message center or using an 'SMS gateway' website. If the phone is switched off or out of range, messages are stored in the network and are delivered at the next opportunity.

SMS was created as part of the Global System for Mobile commu-nications (GSM) Phase 1 Standard, and was originally envisaged for uses such as mobile phone engineers directly transmitting messages to one another without using valuable network minutes. History tells a different story: the resulting text-messaging boom is regarded by many as a precursor to the drive for rich content and services promised by 3G networks.

Why Symbian OS?

These key characteristics of the mobile phone environment – the small size of mobile devices, the requirement to address a mass market, intermittent wireless connectivity, the need for product diversity and an open platform for independent software developers – are the principles upon which an open, advanced operating system must be designed and developed. These considerations make it distinct from any desktop, workstation or server operating system. They also differentiate Symbian OS from embedded operating systems, or any of its competitors, which weren't designed with all these key points in mind.

Supporting industry standards

Symbian OS implements a wide range of communication and other indus-try standards and is adding to these all the time. This section is a quick reference to help readers interested in finding out more about these standards.

Name	Description
Bluetooth	An open specification for seamless wireless short-range communications of data and voice between both mobile and stationary devices See **www.bluetooth.com.**
CDMA	Code division multiple access: a digital wireless telephony transmission technique. The leading standard is IS-95. See **www.tiaonline.org.**
CompactFlash	A storage medium for mobile devices. See **www.compactflash.org.**
GPRS	General packet radio service: a 2.5G radio technology for GSM networks that adds packet-switching protocols and shorter setup time for ISP connections, and offers the potential to charge by amount of data sent rather than connect time. See **www.gsmworld.com.**
GSM	Global system for mobile communications: the most widely-used digital mobile phone system and the wireless telephone standard in Europe. See **www.gsmworld.com.**
HSCSD	High-speed circuit-switched data: a dedicated circuit-switched data communications technology for GSM. See **www.gsmworld.com.**
HTTP	The underlying transfer protocol used by the World Wide Web. See **www.w3.org.**
IMAP4	Internet message access protocol: a highly-functional protocol for retrieving email over the Internet.
IPv4	The traditional Internet protocol standard, which defines addressing and packet formats for communication over the Internet.
IPv6	Extension of the traditional IPv4 standard, enabling a much larger number of address spaces.
IrDA	Infrared Data Association: the standards body that defines a suite of protocols for infrared exchange of data between two devices. See **www.irda.org.**

Name	Description
IrTranP	Infrared Transfer Picture: this provides transfer of pictures from digital cameras to devices over infrared. See **www.irda.org.**
MIDP	Mobile information device profile: a set of Java APIs that is generally implemented on the connected limited device configuration (CLDC). It provides a basic Java 2 Micro Edition (J2ME) application runtime environment targeted at mobile information devices, such as mobile phones and two-way pagers. See **http://java.sun.com/products/midp.**
MultiMediaCard	MMC: An open standard for removable, solid-state memory. See **www.mmca.org.**
POP3	Post Office protocol v3: a common protocol for transferring mail from the server ('Post Office') to the client.
RS232	The standard for serial data transmission using cables.
SMS	Short message service: a GSM service for sending and receiving short text messages. See **www.gsmworld.com.**
SMTP	Simple mail transfer protocol: the commonest protocol employed for transferring Internet mail messages from the client to the server.
SyncML	Synchronization markup language: the outcome of an industry-wide initiative to create a single, common data synchronization protocol optimized for wireless networks. The SyncML Initiative is now part of the Open Mobile Alliance. See **www.openmobilealliance.org/tech/affiliates/ syncml/syncmlindex.html.**
TCP/IP	The Internet communications protocol suite, which supplies the data and transport protocols for higher-level protocols such as web and email.
Unicode	A 16-bit character encoding scheme allowing characters from all major world languages to be encoded in a single character set. See **www.unicode.org.**

Name	Description
USB	Universal serial bus: an external bus standard that supports high data-transfer rates and a single interface for diverse device types. See ***www.usb.org.***
WAP	Wireless application protocol: a set of communication protocol standards to make accessing online services from a mobile phone simple. See ***www.wapforum.org.***

CHAPTER 3

The Roots of Symbian

On 24 June 1998 a new company, Symbian, was announced to the world. It marked the coming together of the world's largest mobile phone manufacturers at that time – Ericsson, Motorola and Nokia – with a leading-edge software company, Psion. Their vision was simple: in the future, mobile phones were going to be used for more than just phone calls – they were going to transmit and manage data. In short, they would have the ability to be the 'remote controls' that we would use to manage our lives, in the same way that the personal computer provided us the means to manage a business from the desktop. To realize this vision, they would need a powerful standards-based software platform, and Symbian would be the company to develop it.

Every mobile phone requires an operating system, the engine that, amongst other things, ensures appropriate information is displayed on the screen for the phone user. For many years, mobile phone manufacturers relied on their own in-house operating systems – these first generation operating systems were not overly costly, managing the interface with the network (allowing you to make a call) and interacting with the user by running basic text menus on small, monochrome screens. While still complex by anyone's standards, it is interesting to note that one of these original operating systems used by a major manufacturer is said to have been developed in the early 1990s by a summer vacation student.

To become 'remote controls for our lives', mobile phones would need to manage more information in a more complex environment. For instance, future mobile phones would include contact lists running to many hundreds of names. Each name would include several addresses, not only for obvious communication channels such as email, pictures and voice, but also for transactions, such as paying for goods and services. The architectural challenge of doing this with a simple operating system might be likened to building a one-storied house and then deciding to add more and more floors. The foundations designed for a one-storied building would not be adequate to support a skyscraper.

New foundations

Psion was a British company which had created a cult following for its powerful digital organizers. The operating system (which was known as EPOC) that powered Psion organizers had been specifically designed for small, handheld devices that were dependent on battery power alone. In the mid-1990s, Psion approached Ericsson and Nokia with its vision for developing the phones of the future. This resulted in several joint development projects being undertaken by the three companies which helped prove that Psion's operating system could indeed make the leap from its niche to a mass-market software platform.

The Psion 5mx is a cult classic with an enthusiastic following. Even today, some Symbian old-timers will not be parted from them

Amazingly, in 1996, the software developers in Psion who developed EPOC numbered less than 80. Productive as this development team was, it was insufficient for EPOC to make the jump to become a major software platform. To enable the world's mobile phone industry to deploy a multitude of devices based on a single operating system, significant investment was required to fund an increase in engineering capacity. The solution was the creation of Symbian, a joint venture which would give shareholders parity to guide the direction of the company, its technology and requirements. Psion contributed the EPOC operating system, which was renamed 'Symbian OS'. Nokia, Ericsson and, later, Motorola contributed the funding.

Growing up

On 24 June 1998, Symbian was officially announced to the world. At the time, it had around 150 employees and was operating out of a small,

Harcourt Street, where it all began, is known as the 'sweetshop'. It is bigger on the inside

unremarkable office in Marylebone, West London. Growth was rapid, with headcount rising to around 200 by the end of 1999 and over 400 by the end of 2001. Meanwhile, Ericsson provided a software development site in Ronneby, Sweden and a new office was opened in Cambridge, UK to take advantage of the technology expertise of the region and at the famous local university. By 2005, the number of employees in Symbian had more than doubled again and a noticeable trend toward establishing a development 'campus' saw a cluster of new offices taken on in London.

It was not just internally that Symbian saw change. In June 1999, a new shareholder, Panasonic, joined the fold providing further funding and exposure to the leading-edge mobile phone market of Japan. Symbian's ethos was embracing the mobile phone world with its concept of an open, advanced mobile phone software platform available to all manufacturers on equal terms.

In many ways, the concept of Symbian embracing all mobile phone manufacturers seems an impossible task. It gathers under a single banner the fiercest commercial competitors who are battling for market share, where competitive advantage can and does make millions of dollars. Yet by engaging with Symbian and sharing its vision, they had agreed to work together toward a common goal. The reason was simple: they recognized that fragmentation of standards would only slow the adoption of advanced mobile phones and the services they delivered.

There are many examples to draw from in the pantheon of consumer electronics. In the 1980s, the introduction of video recorders was consumed by a standards battle between formats. Once the VHS format had become the acknowledged standard, the market took off. Consumers became confident in the knowledge that their videos would work on any recorder they chose to buy and that any recorder they bought would work with their video collection. Similarly, the creation of a single, integrated and standard mobile phone platform would give consumers confidence that their photos and ringtones would work on any phone they bought. Not only that, it would afford the companies a platform to protect their investment, ensuring that, unlike Betamax, the platform they invested in *would* become the standard.

To ensure that Symbian would indeed become the preferred operating system for advanced mobile phones, the use of Symbian OS was not limited to shareholders. The operating system was made available to everyone on equal commercial terms, and an organizational structure was created to ensure that the owners of the company did not exert more influence over the creation of its technology than any other licensee of the product. Very quickly other manufacturers licensed Symbian OS, including Fujitsu, Siemens and Samsung.

The Dot.com boom

The early years of Symbian's existence were influenced quite heavily by the world around it. This was the period when the Internet took off and stock markets around the world hit new highs on the back of the dot.com boom. Symbian did not have much luck insisting that it was not a dot.com company. As a technology company central to the mobile phone revolution, it was swept along in the general hype of the time, driving up expectations to unexpectedly high levels.

The challenge in the early years was to prove the technology worked in a mass-market context and that Symbian could supply huge consumer electronics manufacturing companies in a predictable and timely manner. Once it had achieved that, it would be necessary to prove to these companies that Symbian OS was a viable alternative to the incumbent operating systems.

Originally, Symbian had planned to provide both the underlying operating platform and the user interface (UI). However, it became very difficult to get agreement on a single, common UI that was acceptable to all Symbian OS licensees. Symbian was increasingly being asked to provide more and more alternatives to satisfy the demand for UIs. Debate revolved around screen size and orientation and the use of pen, keys and touch screens. The permutations were endless and as much as some manufacturers wanted them others did not. The software in a phone comprises two major elements: the underlying operating system and the UI. The UI is the part that people see, the part that enables them to interact with their mobile phone and the environment in which it operates. It was apparent that while there was huge value to mobile phone manufacturers in adopting a common underlying operating system, they needed to have control over the look and feel of their products, especially as the opportunity for innovation grew. The UI was as much a part of their offering to their customers as the shape and design of the hardware – a key component of their competitive advantage.

Symbian now has several offices based in Southwark, London

However, Symbian did not have the engineering capacity or funding to undertake development of all of these opportunities. Against the backdrop of a deflated dot.com bubble, Psion, Ericsson, Motorola, Panasonic and Nokia decided to split the UI development from the underlying operating system development. A decision point was reached in May 2001 and Symbian began to focus its attention on creating a common operating system as its licensees took on the task of creating their own user interfaces.

Symbian would continue to develop the core operating system that would be common to all phones. However, the manufacturers would be free to develop or license a UI that would be integrated on top of the operating system. Symbian did in fact continue to develop a UI in-house, known as UIQ, but there was no obligation for manufacturers to take it. The passage of time has led to several commercially available UIs being developed for Symbian OS:

- UIQ – provided by UIQ Technology (now a subsidiary of Symbian) and licensed to several manufacturers
- S60 – developed by Nokia and licensed to several other manufacturers
- Series 80 – developed and used exclusively by Nokia

- A FOMA UI – developed by Fujitsu for NTT DoCoMo in Japan and also available to several other Japanese manufacturers.

Since 2001 Symbian has maintained this strategy and continued to embrace the industry. Around it, the competitive environment has changed. Nokia has become the dominant mobile phone manufacturer selling over 35% of mobile phones worldwide. Samsung has risen to become the third-largest manufacturer, behind Motorola, with over 12% market share. Ericsson, with a declining market share and escalating losses, sold its mobile phone business into a joint venture with Sony in 2001, calling it Sony Ericsson.

Symbian has seen its shareholder base grow several times. In 2002 Sony Ericsson took over as an active licensee and shareholder alongside Ericsson, which had retained its shareholding but no longer licensed the operating system. In 2002 Siemens also joined and, a year later, Samsung added its considerable weight to the companies developing with Symbian OS. In early 2003, Symbian's shareholders and licensees accounted for over three-quarters of all worldwide phone sales.

The second half of 2003 and 2004 saw further changes in ownership as two shareholders left the Symbian consortium. In 2003, Motorola decided to sell its shareholding to Nokia and Psion to better reflect its own platform strategy. In China, Motorola was developing a Linux platform for mobile phones and it felt it could better align its corporate strategy by selling its stake in Symbian and focusing on this multiple platform approach. Whether by art or design, Motorola caused some confusion by choosing to sell its shares the day after it launched its first Symbian OS mobile phone. For Symbian, it was an illustration of Motorola's continued commitment as a Symbian OS licensee and perfectly reflected the egalitarian nature of Symbian's licensing model. Motorola remains an active licensee and has launched several phones using Symbian OS.

Psion chose to sell its shareholding to a combination of other shareholders in 2004. While being quoted on the London Stock Exchange, Psion was a much smaller organization than the other shareholders. In 2001, it took the decision to stop manufacturing the legendary Psion Organiser and no longer intended to build connected mobile devices on Symbian OS. Its Symbian shareholding was primarily a financial investment and, in the absence of any plans to float Symbian on the stock market, Psion decided to sell its stake and realize the value of its investment.

Symbian remains an independent company. While it has very powerful shareholders, no single shareholder has a majority: the shareholders are subject to a Shareholders' Agreement that governs the management of the company. While shareholders have the right to appoint directors, these directors act in much the same way as a non-executive team of directors would act in a public company under an independent chairman.

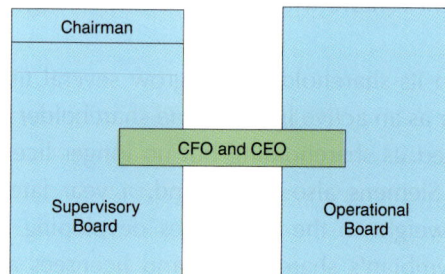

Chairman

CFO and CEO

Supervisory Board

Operational Board

Day-to-day operations are controlled by an operational board of directors managed by the CEO. Operationally, there have been many changes as one would expect from a company that has grown so fast in so few years

In the beginning

Symbian has come a long way from its origins in Marylebone, West London. It now employs over 1000 staff worldwide and there are Symbian offices in ten countries, including the USA, China, Japan and India. Whilst the company remains based in London with its campus-style approach, it has a multicultural ethos, employing staff from more than 40 countries. In 2003, it established a development center in Bangalore and Symbian India now has around 200 people.

Symbian's leaders

Since its foundation, Symbian has employed three CEOs. Symbian OS C++ code written by the first, Colly Myers, can still be found in the operating system today. A driving force in establishing the operating system as a viable mass market mobile phone platform, he helped give it the integrity that meant it was accepted by the phone manufacturers. He left Symbian in 2002 and now runs a small text-messaging company.

With a background in management consultancy, David Levin took over as CEO in April 2002. He was instrumental in raising the profile of Symbian in

Colly Myers

the media and industry as a whole and led the company in a period when its product became the widely accepted mobile phone platform. David left Symbian in early 2005 to take over from Lord Hollick as CEO of United Business Media.

David Levin

Nigel Clifford

Nigel Clifford has taken over as CEO during a period when Symbian has proven its software and has a solid base of partners and customers. The challenges he must address concern the company making the transition from a sales- to a market-led organization and how Symbian OS can penetrate more pervasively into the mobile phone market.

CHAPTER 4

Symbian OS Fundamentals

In previous chapters we examined the characteristics of the mobile phone environment, and the attributes necessary for a mobile phone operating system. In this chapter, we will give you an overview of Symbian OS. It is intended to give you an understanding of the basic structure of the operating system and how it is delivered to customers and partners. The remainder of the chapter is designed to give an overview of some of the common (but often arcane) terms which refer to key features of the operating system.

Symbian OS architecture

Symbian OS is a modular operating system, which means that it is constructed from well defined, discrete parts, each of which contributes particular functionality to the whole. This enables a high degree of configurability of the operating system across a wide range of target hardware.

At a high level, it can be thought of in terms of a layered model, with hardware layers at the bottom and support for user-level applications at the top. In such a model, each layer is thought of as abstracting the services of the layer below into more specialized services for use by higher layers.

Kernel services and hardware interface

At the heart of any operating system is the kernel. The kernel is responsible for managing the hardware resources of the device on which it runs on behalf of the rest of the system, including, at the highest level, user applications. On a modern processor (CPU), the kernel always runs in a special 'privileged' or 'executive' hardware mode.

| UI Framework | UI Application Framework | UI Toolkit | MIDP 2.0 |
| | | | CLDC 1.1 |

(figure)

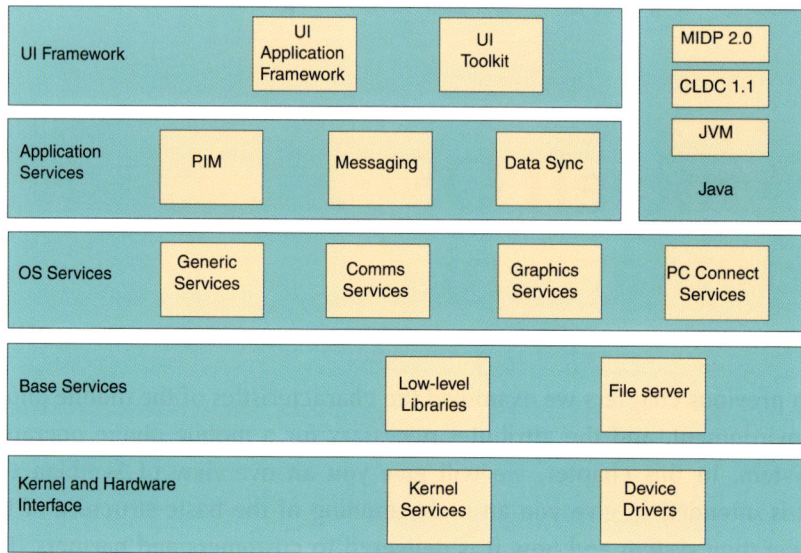

Symbian OS architecture

Symbian OS adopts what is called a nano-kernel design. The kernel is responsible for a very few critical services: principally managing system memory, scheduling programs for execution, and (through individual device drivers) directly managing the interface to device hardware. As far as possible, all other services are run outside the kernel and in a non-privileged, 'user' mode, protecting the kernel from the kinds of errors which plague less well-structured systems and carefully separating application code (both poorly written applications and malware) from the critical operating system services.

Base services

The base services layer supplies the key libraries and frameworks which extend the small, highly specialized kernel into a usable, programmable platform capable of supporting 'middleware' services and other services up to user applications.

For example, the user libraries and file server provide basic facilities expected of any operating system: cryptographic libraries, a database and other persistent storage models, and a host of utility libraries fill out the foundation of the operating system. It is noteworthy that in order to contribute to an overall more robust system, these services are not run inside the privileged kernel, as they would be in many other operating systems.

Kernel

The kernel is the core of an operating system. It manages the machine's hardware resources (including the processor and the memory) and controls the way any other software component can access these resources. The kernel runs with a higher privilege than other programs ('user-mode' programs). The power and robustness of the operating system kernel play a major role in shaping overall system design and reliability.

From version 8.1b onwards Symbian OS contained a real-time kernel. This kernel enables mobile phone manufacturers to build Symbian OS smartphones based on a single core processor where two processors are commonly used today (see Chapter 9). This will lower the cost of creating a smartphone and so give smartphones greater appeal to a larger market.

OS services

The OS services layer supplies the infrastructure for all communications services, multimedia and graphics support, connectivity services, and key libraries such as the C Standard Library which supports porting of applications from other operating systems, and some security-related certificate and cryptographic key libraries.

These services provide the critical infrastructure for a modern smartphone operating system, with support ranging from the latest font and vector graphics open standards to full-scale networking, shortlink (for example, Bluetooth) and, of course, telephony services, including 2G, 2.5G, and 3G support for voice and data.

Application services

The application services layer specializes the generic services supplied by the lower layers of the operating system towards particular classes of application (messaging applications, personal information management (PIM) applications and data synchronization applications) and increasingly also network services (device management and provisioning, for example). It includes support for standards, including SyncML, and application-level Internet and network protocols, including HTTP and WAP.

In general, these services are brokered to user-level applications by UI-specific interfaces supplied by licensees and serve as the common core underlying the custom applications supplied by for example UIQ, S60, and FOMA.

Also included in this layer are the generic data models specialized by UI-level applications, for example, the Contacts and Agenda models.

Applications

Also referred to as 'software', an application is a piece of code written and packaged in such a way as to allow the user to do something. An example of a built-in application is the Agenda in Symbian OS that ships in every smartphone and allows users to manage appointments. Users can also personalize their smartphones by installing their own applications, which can be bought (or downloaded free of charge) from network operators and online retailers.

User interface framework

The UI framework supplies the common core which enables custom UIs to be developed on top of Symbian OS. Generic frameworks free from look-and-feel policies supply the common underlying behavior for all applications, as well as the widget libraries, windowing model, screen furniture (for example, tool bars) and the extension mechanisms used by licensees to create custom UIs.

Unicode

Unicode is a 16-bit character encoding scheme allowing characters from Western European, Eastern European, Cyrillic, Greek, Arabic, Hebrew, Chinese, Japanese, Korean, Thai, Urdu, Hindi and all other major world languages to be encoded in a single character set. The Unicode specification also includes standard compression schemes and a wide range of typesetting information required for worldwide deployment of smartphones.

Symbian OS incorporates Unicode. The use of Unicode is vital to an operating system that is to be used on a global scale as it allows text on the mobile phone to be presented in a region's local language.

Symbian OS technology

Symbian OS is written in the C++ development language. This means that the application programming interfaces (APIs) it exposes to developers are object-oriented. Other operating systems, for example Palm, Windows and Linux, are procedurally based. Object-oriented operating systems are widely regarded as providing major engineering benefits in a mobile environment:

- They require less memory as they support greater code reuse.
- They reduce the overall complexity of the operating system.

While most procedural operating systems provide 'object libraries', the benefits of these are not available to the operating system itself, which means that beneath the object-oriented code there is more code (taking up more memory) and more complexity (taking up engineering time).

C++

C++ is an industry standard object-oriented compiled language. C++ is a general-purpose programming language with a bias towards systems programming. It runs on most computers, from the most powerful supercomputers to personal computers. Symbian OS is written in C++ and it is, therefore, referred to as the 'native' language of the operating system.

The most powerful Symbian OS applications are written in C++. Symbian OS is written in C++ and therefore C++ applications can interact directly with the core functionality of the operating system. For non-native development, Symbian OS also supports a range of other application programming languages (including Java, OPL and Flash). These non-native languages execute in a secure environment on top of Symbian OS and make smartphones available to an even larger group of innovators (see Chapter 11).

Multitasking

A key benefit of Symbian OS is that it is a multitasking operating system, which means that its kernel is able to run multiple programs at the same time. While a smartphone's screen is generally too small to display more than one application at once (in contrast to a desktop PC using Windows, for instance), the smartphone user can still switch between running applications as and when needed.

Also, as with operating systems such as Linux and Windows (and unlike Palm OS), Symbian OS allows multiple 'threads' to execute, even in a single application. Threads are streams of code that run in parallel with one another, based on their priorities (which are decided by the kernel).

Dynamic link libraries

A dynamic link library (DLL) is a library that is loaded into memory when needed and its functions are available to all running programs. It is a vital way of making the most of the limited memory available in a mobile phone, as only one copy of each loaded DLL exists in memory at a time. This is more efficient than a traditional 'static' library, where each application that uses the library's functions links to a separate copy of its code, multiplying the amount of memory used. DLLs are used extensively in Symbian OS and there are well over 100 of them on a typical smartphone.

Client–server architecture

Symbian OS (in common with many other operating systems) is based on a 'client–server architecture'. Generally, you cannot 'see' a server in Symbian OS as it has no user interface but it acts as an engine to manage some resource on behalf of another program. The programs it does this for are known as clients, which are programs that users do see. A simple example of this concept is the web browser on a smartphone – the browser is the client through which the smartphone user receives web pages, but it is the browser's server that makes the physical connection to the Internet.

Symbian OS is not designed as a 'complete' smartphone product – mobile phone manufacturers may develop their own user interface (on-screen menus and graphics) on top of Symbian OS.

Open access and transparency are seen as crucial enablers to mobile phone manufacturers. In all cases, with both Symbian OS and user interfaces, licensees are provided with the underlying source code. The added transparency of being able to see all the way down to the 'nuts-and-bolts' of the operating system greatly assists defect evaluation, error detection, ongoing collaboration and the ability to innovate.

More realistically, many manufacturers now separately license a pre-existing platform and customize it for their own needs. The table below shows the current creators of Symbian OS platforms and the companies that license them (as of March 2005; for regular updates please visit *www.symbian.com*). For more information about these platforms, please see Chapter 6.

User Interface	Supplier	Licensees
S60	Nokia	Nokia, Panasonic, Samsung, Lenovo, LG
UIQ	UIQ (an independent, wholly owned subsidiary of Symbian)	Sony Ericsson, Motorola, BenQ, Arima
FOMA UI	NTT DoCoMo	Fujitsu, Mitsubishi, Sharp, Sony Ericsson

Memory in Symbian OS

Memory is scarce in the mobile phone environment, mainly due to battery and size constraints, and mobile phones need to make good use of the small amounts of memory they possess. Various types of memory exist on Symbian OS smartphones:

- Random Access Memory (RAM) is used by running programs. Applications vary in how much RAM they need, and this also depends on what the application is doing at the time. For example, a browser application loading a web page needs to allocate more RAM for the web page data as it is loaded. The more RAM you have, the more programs you can run on a smartphone at any time. Typically, smartphones have between 7 and 30 MB of RAM available.
- Read Only Memory (ROM) is where you will find Symbian OS. It includes all startup code, device drivers and other hardware-specific code. This

area cannot be used for storage, although it can be seen in the phone file system as drive Z:. If you view the Z: drive, it will show all the built-in applications of Symbian OS, as well as system DLLs, device drivers and system configuration files. For added memory efficiency, code in ROM is executed in place, which means it is not loaded into RAM before executing. Typically a smartphone has between 16 and 32 MB of ROM.

- Internal Flash memory acts like a disk drive and allows files to be both read from and written to it via the Symbian OS file system. The file system has a hierarchical directory structure, with very similar features to those you would find on, say, a desktop PC. The internal Flash drive is represented as the C: drive on a smartphone. This memory contains applications loaded by the user, as well as data such as documents, pictures, video, bookmarks and calendar entries. The amount of internal Flash memory available varies with the phone, but it can be quite generous. For example, the Nokia 9500 has 80 MB of internal Flash memory available.

- Memory cards act as removable disk drives and allow you to supplement built-in storage. You can read from and write to a memory card just like the internal disk, including operations such as saving user data and even installing applications. This card is treated as another disk volume by the file system and is represented by another drive letter, such as D: or E:. Memory cards formats (MMC and SD are common examples) vary as does the amount of memory you can buy, from 16 MB (or less) all the way up to 1 GB.

Kernel

The Symbian OS kernel consists of a set of executables and data files which run in the CPU's privileged mode and provide basic system management and control. The kernel handles the creation and scheduling of threads and processes. In addition, the kernel manages all the system memory, and acts as a gateway that provides access to device hardware.

The kernel is divided in a way such that the bulk of the kernel code is abstracted from the hardware (which means it is written so that the specifics of the hardware do not matter). Through the kernel, software can load and use device drivers. Device drivers primarily control specific hardware peripherals such as communications ports, radio modems, and external

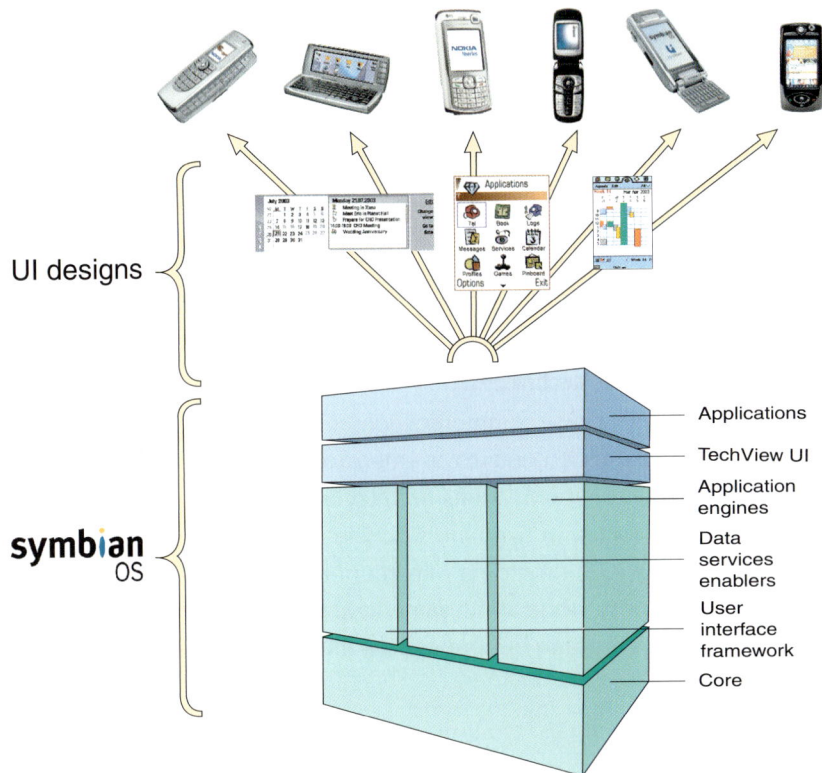

The layers of Symbian OS and the user interface designs that sit on top

storage devices. The kernel implements the functions for user programs to load and communicate with device drivers.

UI architecture

To understand the architectural rationale of Symbian OS, consider the two extremes a mobile phone manufacturer can choose in selecting software for their smartphone. At one extreme, it can create its own operating system, but this results in extensive development costs and little or no software being available. At the other extreme, the manufacturer can choose an operating system with a complete, built-in user interface. The advantages of this include low development cost in implementing the smartphone, as well as having more independently-developed applications to run on it. The disadvantage is that there is little product differentiation since it will be very similar to other phones using that operating system.

The Symbian OS UI architecture provides a balance between these extremes, by having a powerful, common UI 'core' with a flexible architecture that enables the addition of a custom-built user interface. As a result, a mobile phone manufacturer gets a fully featured operating system (they do not have to implement their own) and the flexibility to differentiate their product by developing their own user interfaces. While it is true that Symbian OS applications written for one user interface will not directly run on another, it is fairly easy to port between UIs – for example, from UIQ to S60 – since the main complexity is in the common UI framework code.

The communications architecture

A flexible and powerful communications architecture is vital for smart-phones, and Symbian OS contains an extensive and flexible communications architecture. The communications architecture is a good example of how software is constructed in Symbian OS. The architecture supports different protocols and devices, providing maximum power and flexibility for communications support, while at the same time providing a common interface not only to the application but throughout the various lower system levels.

Symbian OS also includes 'multi-homing' capability, which is the ability to have multiple connections – each with its own Internet address – active at the same time. This is very desirable if you want multiple functions to be active simultaneously that use different GPRS connections (such as MMS and web browsing, for example). Another example is being able to use a wireless office LAN and GPRS at the same time. Multi-homing opens up many possibilities for devices that support multiple ways of accessing the Internet and will become more and more important in future smartphones.

Delivering Symbian OS

Because every mobile phone user has different needs, Symbian OS is designed to support innovation and customization by its licensees and partners. To enable this process, Symbian delivers its product in the following ways:

Symbian OS customization kit

This product is designed for Symbian's licensees, the mobile phone manufacturers. The Customization Kit enables Symbian OS C++ development (with additional Java and assembler support) and includes a test emulator, documentation, examples and full source code. It provides the basic materials for:

- smartphone creation
- creation of UI software development kits (SDKs) for service and application developers.

Symbian OS development kit
This family of products is designed for independent 'pre-platform' developers, enabling them to add valuable new technologies to licensees' smartphone products. It provides the basic materials for third parties to develop technologies for licensees and integrate these technologies into smartphones during their creation.

Development kits give Symbian partners access to a subset of the Symbian OS code available in the Customization Kit, with similar access to Java and assembler support, a test emulator, documentation and examples.

A basic test emulator (known as TechView) and common operating system applications are provided to support the development of smartphones and key technologies. UI designs, reference boards, integrated development environments (IDEs) and debuggers are provided by the Symbian ecosystem, and are discussed throughout this book.

CHAPTER 5

From Feature Phones to Smartphones

Before anyone had even used the word *smartphone*, the ability to add and customize features was driving growth in the mobile phone market. Nokia's emergence in the late 1990s as the world's leading mobile phone manufacturer has been widely attributed to three key factors: compelling handset design, intuitive user interface design, and support for user personalization.

Mobile phone manufacturers saw that mobile phones were highly personal items that were as much fashion statements as they were tools for communication. Nokia, a pioneer of this new market, introduced *Xpress-on* covers, which allowed users to alter the physical appearance of their mobile phones. It also led support for ringtone downloads, enabling users to choose from a limitless – and quite often excruciating – variety of tunes to make their mobile phones stand out from the crowd. The result was not only accelerating market share for Nokia (in particular), but a thriving market for third parties and rapidly growing traffic across mobile networks, as users downloaded increasing numbers of ringtones and logos. The *feature phone* was born.

What makes smartphones different from these traditional feature phones in terms of the flexibility for customization that they offer? Broadly speaking, a smartphone allows richer and deeper levels of customization than a feature phone. The benefits extend to all members of the mobile phone community – it delivers choice to end users, to mobile phone manufacturers at the time of product creation, and to mobile phone network operators while the product is being defined, and even after the mobile phone has been delivered into the hands of subscribers.

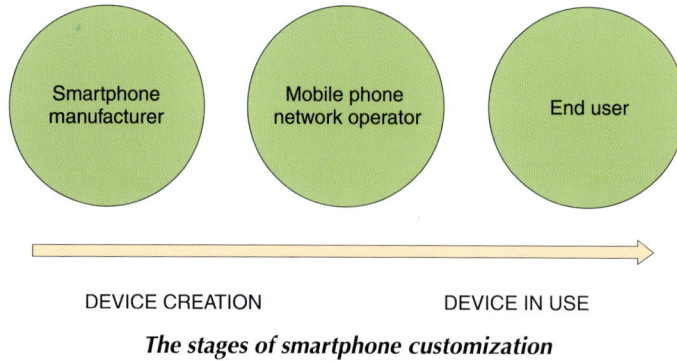

The stages of smartphone customization

With a smartphone, platform customization of the mobile phone experience occurs at three stages. First, the mobile phone manufacturer takes the smartphone software suite and adapts it by adding its own branding and extra applications. Secondly, during the device shipping and deployment phase, the mobile phone network operator adds its customizations. This can happen at the factory late in the production process, in the warehouse or the shop through the addition of memory cards packed with operator-specific applications, or, once the device is in the field, via over-the-air (OTA) provisioning. Finally, the end user has the opportunity to change, personalize and customize the mobile phone throughout its lifetime in the field, by downloading applications, subscribing to new services, and creating their own content, such as videos and photographs, and using these to give the mobile phone a unique personality.

Customization by mobile phone manufacturers

Mobile phone manufacturers want a software platform that helps them to face emerging business needs. To provide ever more innovative mobile phone designs and features and drive growth in a market that in many parts of the world has reached 100% penetration (or more), they need to streamline the way they create products.

With the traditional 'vertically-integrated' model of mobile phone creation, manufacturers develop hardware and software, all the way from low-level processing, right up to the user interface, application features and handset design. But this model means that each mobile phone manufacturer has to invest considerable research and development effort in solving the same technical problems that its competitors are solving. Furthermore, many of those lower layers of a mobile phone are defined by standards (for example, the

W-CDMA standard for 3G mobile phones), so while they represent a technical challenge, they are destined to be commodity components. Smartphone platforms allow mobile phone manufacturers to outsource the problem.

By licensing an operating system that already provides working telephony, multimedia, messaging functions, a host of applications and a rich user interface (such as UIQ or S60), the manufacturer is able to concentrate its research and development and investments on higher-value activities. These higher-value activities are the ones that *differentiate* – that help to expand market share – and involve adapting and customizing the platform in order to meet specific market needs.

Precise targeting of market segments

The most advanced mobile phone markets, such as those of South Korea and Japan, are notable for a vast proliferation of mobile phone designs. If you take a walk through Tokyo's 'Electronics Town', Akihabara, you will discover a bewildering variety of models, from retro 'candybar' designs with 1980s-style displays, to the latest slimline 'clamshells', most of which offer TV, video recording and music on the move. These mobile phones compete on features, fashion and design, in a market where new competitors appear on an almost weekly basis. Features move at an astonishing pace – a new model is barely available for more than a month or two before it is considered old-fashioned.

Inevitably in such circumstances, the average lifespan of a mobile phone design dwindles. The consequence of this for manufacturers is that they need to produce more products more quickly. To remain competitive, mobile phone manufacturers must find ways of enabling shorter production runs of devices with lower development costs for each new design. Mobile phone manufacturers are turning to third-party software platforms in order to address their needs. Smartphone platforms are designed to be flexible and to allow the easy addition or adaptation of features. They enable the mobile phone manufacturer to create a common 'chassis' from which they can derive a whole range of mobile phone designs with different looks, features and target markets. This approach allows manufacturers to target new customer segments as well as keep up with the demands of a fashion-conscious market.

In 2004, Fujitsu demonstrated the flexibility of the smartphone platform in Japan when it launched a Symbian OS smartphone targeting elderly users.

The F880i ES was outwardly a new concept in mobile phone design – a simplified user interface, larger than usual keypad buttons, and a set of shortcut keys for dialing the top three contact numbers. But beneath the surface, the F880i ES shared the same design as the more advanced range of smartphones Fujitsu had launched on the NTT DoCoMo network. What enabled Fujitsu to create a low-volume variant, targeting a highly specific market segment was its ability to reuse a common underlying chassis – Symbian OS – with only superficial modifications to the user interface and industrial design.

The F880i ES was built by Fujitsu for NTT DoCoMo, successfully targeting a new market segment of elderly users

From hardware to software

The most obvious way that mobile phone manufacturers differentiate their products is in the physical design – or form factor – of their mobile phones. The software components of a mobile phone continue to grow in significance as the requirement to be able to differentiate models shows no sign of abating. The past few years have delivered an explosion in creative design as the introduction of new technology – such as cameras, hard disks, video-calling, and email – has led to ever increasing experimentation with new industrial design concepts. A market that used to consist of either the 'candybar' or the 'clamshell' design now offers mobile phones with sliding or swiveling displays, dedicated music controls, QWERTY keyboards, pen input, twisting displays in the style of mini-camcorders, and any number of design permutations in between.

Can a software platform help a mobile phone manufacturer in their quest to produce winning hardware designs? Yes it can, by offering flexibility in how it handles data input and output. Symbian OS is designed and built to enable every conceivable (and some as yet inconceivable) method of user input – keypad, keyboard, pen, voice, jogdial, joystick – and to support a variety of screen sizes. The user interface platforms that have been developed for Symbian OS, such as S60 and UIQ, go even further, allowing easy transition of applications between different modes of input (you might use a keypad with S60 and a pen with UIQ) or orientation of display.

The second, and somewhat more recent, phase of product differentiation for mobile phone manufacturers is in the software itself. Traditional mobile phones with in-house operating systems were so limited in functionality and user experience that the opportunities for differentiation were few.

Mozzies shipped on the Siemens SX1, demonstrating the exciting and innovative possibilities of an open platform by blending 'live' background images with addictive game-play

However, open operating systems provide mobile phone manufacturers with a new platform with which they can compete. Innovative applications are becoming a significant means of catching the public's imagination. Examples include innovative use of the built-in camera to provide a 'live' game background in the Siemens 'Mozzies' game, and Nokia's LifeBlog – an application which enables users to get more value from the functionality in a particular line of smartphones, by creating a shareable online diary derived from the pictures and messages a user captures on their mobile phone.

Customization by network operators

Mobile network operators have traditionally struggled to differentiate themselves to mobile phone users. This is partly because many users choose the mobile phone they want before they choose the network; mobile phone brand and design is often foremost in the user's mind when making a purchasing decision. Network operators have addressed this to a degree with special deals and shrewd promotion, such as Vodafone's exclusive Sharp GX series of mobile phones, which were among the first to feature the Vodafone Live! branding.

However, the biggest obstacle in the race for customer loyalty was the fact that for many years the services on offer were so simple that they did not differ much from one network operator to the next. Mobile phones were just telephones, terminals for accessing a voice network. For a customer, placing a voice call with one network operator was very much like placing a voice call with another. It was necessary then to differentiate, if an operator was to build brand loyalty and avoid losing subscribers to rival networks.

Smartphones offer network operators a platform for delivering greater innovation and greater differentiation. This is not before time. With voice call revenues in long-term decline, and most markets reaching a point where there are few new subscribers to be found, network operators are in need of new ways to control costs and sustain growth. By adopting and customizing a common smartphone platform across their range of mobile phones, they are finding strategies for achieving these goals.

A common platform

If every phone on a mobile phone network has a different user interface, a different screen size and a different programming environment, what are the impacts? First, network sales and support staff must be trained to support every single model. Secondly, all content produced by the network operator (for example, a news page on its portal) must be tested and 'repurposed' for every mobile phone, perhaps even across multiple programming languages (we cover programming languages in more detail in Chapter 11). And thirdly, any application that the operator has created in order to provide access to new services (for example, a music player application that can download new tracks) will need to be re-developed for each mobile phone. Now multiply this effort by the 40 or so new models that a typical network operator might introduce each year, the many language variants they must carry, and the dozens of mobile phones still being used on their network purchased over the previous few years. The implication is clear: a diverse device population based on different standards presents painful cost barriers to launching any new service.

Platform

A platform is a set of technologies which act as a foundation for applications or higher-level platforms. Symbian OS includes C++ APIs, a leading Java implementation, an application suite and integration with wireless and other communications protocols as a platform for smartphone creation.

Developers create applications and services for UI platforms (such as S60 and UIQ) based on Symbian OS. Network operators use Symbian OS as a platform for deploying applications and services. Mobile phone manufacturers use Symbian OS as a platform to develop families of smartphones that utilize the same underlying hardware but have variations in design and functionality.

Smartphones help network operators overcome these challenges. They deliver a common software platform that can be used across a large proportion of the devices deployed by an operator. At the same time they actually extend the innovative product design that is necessary to meet evolving user requirements. Network operators can drive down their costs by:

- Developing once and deploying many times: new content or applications enabling users to access operator services can be built with a single development language for a standard user interface and deployed across a large footprint of the operator's device population.

- Managing many devices with a single infrastructure: configuring a user's mobile phone, diagnosing and fixing problems, and providing OTA updates to the mobile phone's functionality can all be taken care of with one system, no matter how different the models may appear to the end user.
- Reducing the testing and verification burden: every mobile phone goes through an arduous and rigorous network testing process before it is released by a network operator. As devices become more complex the cost of testing grows. If mobile phones are based on the same platform, the cost of approving them is reduced dramatically.

OTA device management

Over-the-air device management allows either an individual or a network operator to make changes to the software setup or configuration of a mobile phone, by 'pushing' a configuration update to the mobile phone via a wireless link. This eliminates the need for docking the mobile phone or going through an elaborate synchronization process and can allow for implementation of upgrades, software distribution, the running of diagnostics and content delivery.

It is important to stress that OTA, by its nature, applies to configurations done to the mobile phone 'behind the scenes'. Users do not have to actively 'pull' information to their mobile phones – updates 'just happen' in the background without the need for user intervention. A key application of OTA is to allow network operators to update or repair the software on a mobile phone without requiring the physical presence of the mobile phone.

An open platform

As voice call revenues fall relative to the number of subscribers, network operators seek to generate new revenues through new services. But just as important as developing the services themselves is ensuring that they become available as quickly as possible. The slow uptake of Multimedia Messaging Service (MMS) was largely because operators had to migrate their entire customer base from basic to multimedia-enabled mobile phones. This taught the industry that separating the process of developing and deploying services from the much longer process of developing and deploying mobile phones would bring considerable benefits.

Network operators require two key things to accelerate the process of service deployment:

- An open and extensible platform: it is far cheaper and more efficient to deploy a new service solution to a mobile phone the user already owns, than to persuade (and often subsidize) the user to replace the mobile phone itself. Smartphone platforms provide a framework for operators to deploy new solutions or upgrade the operating system, before – or even after – sale.
- A platform with an active development community creating solutions: network operators are not software publishers, nor do they necessarily want to be. Instead, they seek to capitalize on their ability to deliver content and their intimate knowledge of their subscribers' needs by engaging with an industry that is spontaneously creating new ideas and can develop solutions to order.

MMS

Based on the same principles as its evolutionary precursor SMS (Short Message Service), Multimedia Messaging Services involves the transmission of images, video clips, sound files and text messages over a wireless network. Designed specifically for 3G networks (and beyond), MMS allows for the quick delivery of varied, content-rich information to a multimedia-enabled device.

Designed to be customized

Network operators actively promote appropriate services to their subscribers and make sure that the discovery of new functions is a pleasure for the user, rather than an ordeal. They aim to do this chiefly by customizing the mobile phone experience itself. One aspect of this is cosmetic and digital branding such as the use of icons and color schemes, which are implemented to remind the user which network they are using. A potentially more rewarding form of customization is where the operator embeds its service access points *within* the mobile phone, either in the 'home' screen or in the menu.

Smartphone platforms are designed for the addition of new applications and enhancement of the basic features you would find when you take a new mobile phone fresh from being built and actually use it for the first time. This type of operator customization is now becoming commonplace in smartphone development. Typically, network operators now:

- specify customization requirements to their mobile phone suppliers, such as what information and links appear on the 'home' screen, the look-and-feel, and the text labels and icons that the user sees
- work with independent software developers to build unique applications that mobile phone manufacturers will include in their phones. This allows the operator to build highly customized variants of standard mobile phones – enabling them to differentiate themselves without paying the price of a completely tailor-made solution.

Orange is extremely active with independent developers and the solutions it deploys are critical to its relationship with its customers

- update smartphones over the air. With the right customizations made to the mobile phone during manufacture, operators can subsequently promote new services to the user's 'home' screen. Examples include delivering new applications and updating catalogs of available services direct to a subscriber's mobile phone – a big change in service delivery over traditional, closed mobile phones.

Customization by end users

End users have always taken advantage of new ways to customize and personalize their mobile phones. This kind of cosmetic customization has continued to develop as mobile phones have become more advanced. A few years ago, users began downloading logos to display in the mobile phone's home screen. Advanced platforms such as Symbian OS also allow users to download and use not only video clips or pictures as wallpaper, but whole 'skins' that transform the appearance of the mobile phone. Reflecting their huge popularity, ringtones have moved on too: now there are downloadable 'truetones' (real music tracks used as ringtones) and video ringtones, which play video clips as well as sound while the mobile phone is ringing.

True smartphones allow the end user to take personalization a step further. With a smartphone, users can add new applications and whole new suites of functionality, transforming their mobile phone into a unique and highly personal tool that is adapted to their lifestyle. A mobile phone might become a business productivity tool in one user's hands, an in-car navigation system for another, and a multimedia and gaming center for someone else.

The open nature of smartphone platforms has created a thriving economy based around add-on software. Symbian OS mobile phone users can choose from thousands of downloadable applications – available through their network operator's portal, through a catalog on the mobile phone itself, or from websites such as Handango. As the rich choice provided by the mobile industry continues to grow, so too does the individuality and personal value of each subscriber's mobile phone.

The market decides

It is clear that tensions may arise when the various aspects of customization discussed in this chapter are all in play. What happens when the mobile phone manufacturer wants to include one music player application and the network operator wants to include another? What happens if the network operator has one view of how the mobile phone experience should look and the user has another? To a degree this is the nature of an open platform: since the level of flexibility is almost limitless, the market will decide what level is appropriate and desirable. Network operators will choose to promote devices they believe offer differentiation and compelling feature sets, while end users will choose mobile phones that allow them to express their individuality and connect to their preferred online services. Ultimately, the needs of each of these participants – as we will discover in Part II – will accelerate the uptake of flexible smartphone platforms.

The Smartphone Ecosystem

In Part I, we introduced concepts, motives and history that led to the formation of Symbian and the development of an open, industry standard smartphone operating system, Symbian OS. In Part II, we take a closer look at the ecosystem that surrounds Symbian OS. The success of Symbian OS is based on collaborative development. The ecosystem that contributes to the development of smartphones is therefore extremely significant. The end-to-end delivery of smartphones by Symbian, mobile phone manufacturers, network operators, software and content providers is often referred to as a 'value chain'. Yes, yet another industry buzzword, but in the case of smartphones, this chain delivers the building blocks of success.

It is worth reiterating the distinction between *ownership* of Symbian and *licensing* of Symbian OS. Manufacturers that license Symbian OS as a platform for smartphones are referred to as 'Symbian OS licensees'. These licensees account for over three-quarters of global mobile phone shipments, creating a massive industry opportunity to collaborate and define the common standard for smartphones.

In fact, the word 'Symbian' itself represents 'a relationship of mutual benefit or dependence' and, as the name suggests, the company is structured such that an independent, yet collaborative pooling of the most talented technical resources can work together to provide the smartphone platform, not only through its shareholders and licensees, but in tandem with the whole of the mobile phone industry.

In Part II, we look at the key contributors to this 'value chain' and look at their relationships with Symbian. The mobile phone industry expands before our eyes and the complexity of the inter-relationships between software vendors, hardware builders, operators, and developers grows by the day. This ever-expanding cycle of growth and development forms the 'virtuous cycle', shown below.

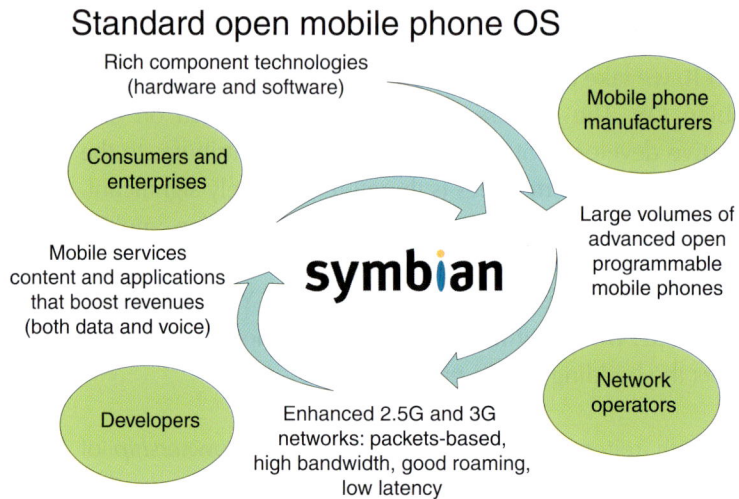

Standard open mobile phone OS

Rich component technologies
(hardware and software)

Consumers and enterprises

Mobile phone manufacturers

Large volumes of advanced open programmable mobile phones

symbian

Mobile services content and applications that boost revenues (both data and voice)

Developers

Enhanced 2.5G and 3G networks: packets-based, high bandwidth, good roaming, low latency

Network operators

The smartphone market virtuous cycle

As mobile phone manufacturers ship tens of millions of open Symbian OS smartphones, network operators are able to derive greater revenue by introducing new network services that will allow people to use their smartphones for an increasing range of everyday activities. Independent software developers engage in this new opportunity by creating products which serve new consumer and business needs. Consumers and enterprises then begin to actively want to use such products and drive demand for open phones which can help them be more productive. What is established is a virtuous cycle, where everyone benefits as the market grows.

An open operating system is essential to drive the capabilities of smartphones into the future. Symbian OS drives standards for the interoperation of smartphones with mobile networks, content applications and services, enterprises, hardware vendors and Symbian developers. In Part II, you can read about what these key innovators contribute to the smartphone industry.

CHAPTER 6

Mobile Phone Manufacturers

Mobile phone networks are in the process of migrating to 3G. As a result, network operators require feature-rich smartphones capable of supporting the wide range of revenue-generating services that will repay their investment in 3G infrastructure. To satisfy the demands of these customers, mobile phone manufacturers must create flexible smartphone platforms which will require an advanced operating system to handle the technical complexity that they contain. It is preferable for this operating system to be open as it enables users to add new applications that can generate further revenues for network operators. Symbian OS is such an operating system and is licensed by the world's leading mobile phone manufacturers.

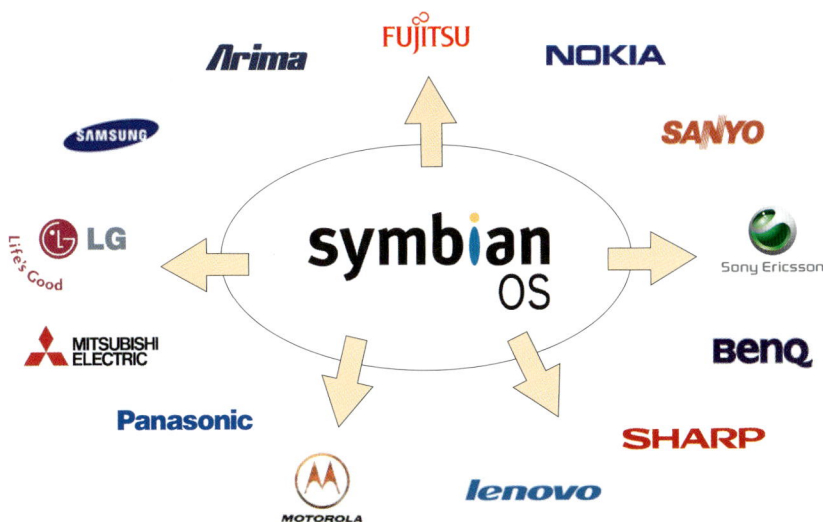

Mobile phone manufacturers licensing Symbian OS (2005)

As discussed in detail in the first part of this book, Symbian was formed in 1998 by mobile phone manufacturers to develop an advanced, open, standard operating system designed specifically for smartphones. It was realized that a powerful mobile phone operating system would become necessary as the complexity of the mobile phone environment increased. Sharing the development cost of creating this operating system, manufacturers could at the same time lead the way in creating a standard (ensuring the interoperability of both their products and the services running on them, and so helping the mobile phone market to expand).

The first mass-market Symbian OS mobile phone was built by Ericsson. This first phone, the R380, offered a large screen with various ways of accessing user information (flip open, flip closed, and a large landscape touch screen). It included a powerful, integrated address book, diary and agenda, however, it was not a smartphone as we define it in this book. While it was a mobile phone that contained a powerful operating system, it was not possible for independent developers to add their applications – an important facet of a smartphone. However, this product proved the viability and value of Symbian OS as a platform.

The Ericsson R380 saw several versions released and proved that Symbian OS was a viable platform for mobile phone manufacturers

The Ericsson R380 was soon followed by the Nokia 9210 Communicator. The Nokia Communicator series had a heritage as a popular professional mobile phone-cum-PDA (earlier iterations of the 9000 Communicator had been built by Nokia using GEOS, a less powerful operating system). The Nokia 9210 included a QWERTY keyboard and a large color screen, and was the first open smartphone on Symbian OS. It was also based on a standard user interface, the Nokia Series 80 platform.

The Nokia 9210 was the first mobile phone that allowed applications to be developed for Symbian OS and was based on the Nokia Series 80 platform

For purists, the first 'real' smartphone was the Nokia 7650, a one-hand-operated mobile phone with a keypad slider, which packed an enormous amount of power and functionality within its small form. It also included another important – and now common – feature of mobile phones, a camera with a reasonable amount of memory for pictures. This was the first mobile phone with the opportunity for customization and new applications. An example of innovation by the community was the swift availability of video recording software.

There has been a steady flow of mobile phone manufacturers licensing and successfully creating phones based on Symbian OS. As of 2005, 60 different mobile phone models had been created based upon Symbian OS and 50 million have been sold. This should not disguise the fact that the mobile phone industry presents a highly competitive marketplace, where change is the rule rather than the exception. For instance, in 2001, Symbian licensee Ericsson announced massive financial losses caused by poor sales of mobile phones. To recover from this Ericsson merged its mobile phone business

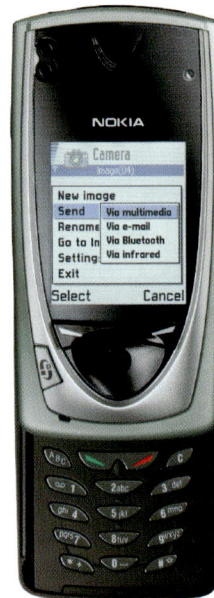

The Nokia 7650 was compact, advanced and ... the first open smartphone

with Sony to form Sony Ericsson. In 2002 Sony Ericsson licensed Symbian OS and has since produced the highly successful P series of mobile phones. Sendo's intellectual property and research and development team was bought by Motorola in 2005 and Siemens mobile was acquired by BenQ.

The Sony Ericsson P800, the first of the successful P series

The value of cooperation

By the end of 2006, the research and development investment in Symbian OS will be approaching US$500 million and this continues to accelerate. Including the user interface platforms that Symbian OS supports (S60, Series 80, UIQ and FOMA UI), the cumulative technology investment in Symbian OS and products is in the order of US$1 billion and it is likely to amount to several times this over the next five years.

The investments that mobile phone manufacturers would need to make to replicate Symbian's efforts imply that a proprietary approach to operating systems is prohibitively expensive for even the largest manufacturers. In the long term, a strategy based on using only proprietary operating systems makes little economic sense.

Other business models, such as open source, exist and these have been used successfully by hardware manufacturers in the server and personal computer product areas. Open source software has non-restrictive licensing terms with the attraction of being royalty-free. However, it still requires an equivalent and massive research and development investment by highly competent engineers. In addition, funding is required from industry benefactors. In the highly competitive world of mobile phones, it is an unlikely proposition.

The current Symbian license fee is US$5 or US$7.25 per unit, depending on the number of mobile phones sold. As the component costs for smartphones converge in a downward trend toward US$100, the Symbian license fee will still only represent less than 5% of manufacturing cost, equivalent to a 30-minute mobile phone call in most countries. As a result, Symbian OS represents value to the mobile phone manufacturer.

As well as the complexity introduced by next-generation mobile telephony standards and services, supporting a mobile phone in an industry which requires end-to-end systems to achieve 'five nines' reliability (99.999%) drives further requirements.

As other operating systems seek to migrate into the smartphone space from personal computer and PDA heritage, the pedigree of Symbian OS and its technological superiority have given it a clear advantage and significant market leadership. Other smartphone software vendors have struggled to meet the increased expectations that users have of their mobile phone and have tended to succeed only by providing niche solutions.

It is, therefore, not surprising that Symbian OS is used in more than double the number of smartphone variants as all other smartphone operating systems combined. This represents an order of magnitude more than Symbian's nearest competitor and demonstrates how significantly fit-for-purpose Symbian OS has become.

A platform for value

Aside from the tangible financial benefit to Symbian of royalties paid by mobile phone manufacturers that license and ship Symbian OS smartphones, intangible benefits are the global and practical insight into the mobile phone industry obtained by pooling the requirements of such a broad range of stakeholders. Licensees are generally comfortable with sharing their planned roadmaps, technology requirements and priorities for the mobile phone industry with Symbian due to the high level of mutual trust. These requirements are used to define the evolution of Symbian OS, contributing to the ongoing usefulness and value of Symbian OS. Symbian OS smartphones are the most innovative and have typically been the first smartphones to take mass numbers of consumers into new service areas. A mobile phone presents one of the most complex engineering challenges and, like all good technology, Symbian OS totally disguises this complexity from the smartphone user.

Symbian's business model allows licensing terms that provide mobile phone manufacturers tremendous flexibility to differentiate and retain brand value. Symbian OS does not seek to compete and, in fact, encourages the proliferation of mobile phone manufacturers' brands. While other smartphone operating systems can create brand conflict with either mobile phone manufacturers or mobile network operators, Symbian OS does not. With billions of dollars invested by mobile phone manufacturers in building their brand identities, Symbian's strategy is to provide an enabling technology and to allow mobile phone manufacturers to use their names to target appropriate market segments. Mobile phones are fashion items and branding matters to their users.

As a technology platform provider, Symbian is not visible to the consumer and it does not need to impose onerous constraints on mobile phone manufacturers to manage how it is perceived by consumers. By not threatening to encroach on other parts of the value chain or even introduce disruptive business models that may capture or bypass parts of the value chain, Symbian receives a high degree of trust and commitment from mobile phone manufacturers.

As in the PC market, the business models of pure smartphone operating system software providers require that hardware becomes a commodity in order that as much value as possible is captured in the underlying software. The hardware commoditization model is driven by the creation of unbranded smartphones, generally manufactured in Asia. These contrasting models of hardware manufacturing exist side-by-side in the mobile market. Brands such as Nokia, Sony Ericsson and Samsung remain huge differentiators with enormous customer loyalty, but there are also many examples of mobile phone manufacturers building phones exclusively for network operators to allow them to build customer loyalty of their own (for instance, Sharp built feature phones exclusively branded for Vodafone). Some Symbian licensees employ a mixture of these production models and it is certainly not within the scope of this book to predict how the market might evolve!

A platform for smartphones (user interfaces)

Symbian OS is not designed to be a complete smartphone product – mobile phone manufacturers may develop their own on-screen menus and graphics (user interface) on top of Symbian OS or, as is more realistic, they may separately license an existing user interface.

Smartphones with a numeric keypad

Smartphones with a numeric keypad are designed for one-handed use and need to be simple to navigate. Such smartphones feature a joystick, keys, jogdial, or any combination of these.

S60

The S60 platform is developed by Nokia, and was first seen in 2001 with the announcement of the hugely successful Nokia 7650. The number and variety of phones launched since then is large and growing quickly, not least because Nokia has licensed the S60 UI to several other major mobile phone manufacturers, including Panasonic, Samsung and Siemens. The latest version of S60 is even more flexible and configurable to different devices, screen sizes and input mechanisms.

Receiving an SMS on S60

FOMA software platform

In Japan, NTT DoCoMo has developed a UI for FOMA phones. Fujitsu, Sharp, Sony Ericsson and Mitsubishi are among DoCoMo's partners developing smartphones on this platform. The FOMA software platform is designed to enable seamless delivery of advanced services on the DoCoMo network, and includes pen-based capabilities, creating new possibilities for users and application developers.

A customized FOMA user interface as available on the FOMA SH700i

Smartphones with touch screens

Touch-screen smartphones tend to have larger screens than those with a numeric keypad and can even dispense with the keypad. Touch screens are ideal for viewing content and working on the move. The addition of a pen to the user input options (alongside the keypad and keyboard) gives new opportunities to users and developers.

UIQ

The UIQ platform is a media-rich customizable open platform, licensed to Arima, BenQ, Motorola and Sony Ericsson. It has proved a hit with smartphones like the Sony Ericsson series, which incorporate various means of data input. Most recent versions of this platform offer one-handed, keyboard and pen-based configurations. UIQ is developed by UIQ Technology, an independent subsidiary of Symbian.

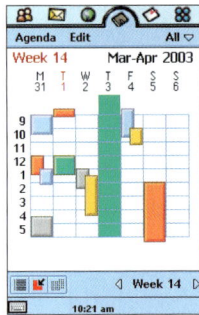

Using the calendar on UIQ as available on the Sony Ericsson P910

Smartphones with full keyboards

Smartphones with full keyboards are designed primarily to provide enterprise and professional users with the best experience possible for accessing, viewing and manipulating data and media content.

Series 80

Series 80 implements a two-handed QWERTY keyboard. Nokia launched its first Series 80 smartphone, the Nokia 9210, in 1999. The UI was the basis of the Nokia 9200 Series and was used in the Nokia 9290 (US version) and Nokia 9210i (improved version). The current generations are the Nokia

Bands

From time to time you hear 'dual-band', 'tri-band' and even 'quad-band' being used to describe a mobile phone's roaming capabilities. Different areas of the globe, for technical and historical reasons, use different frequency bands for their mobile phone networks: for instance, GSM850/GSM 1900 is used in North America and GSM900/GSM 1800 in Europe. Both bands are used in different parts of South America. For a mobile phone to be able to roam seamlessly between these areas, it must be able to operate on an appropriate selection of these bands.

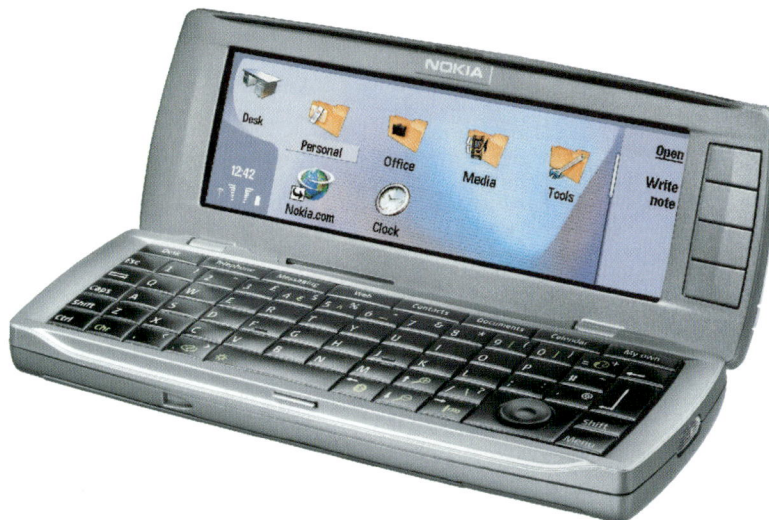

Using the calendar on Series 80 as available on the Nokia 9500

9300 and 9500. Nokia does not currently license Series 80 to any other mobile phone manufacturer.

A platform for extensibility

Increasingly, mobile phone manufacturers are also shipping mobile phones with pre-installed applications from specialist independent software vendors (ISVs). This allows manufacturers yet another tier of customization: smartphones with similar hardware features can be differentiated by software functionality.

Could PDAs, music players, digital cameras and electronic wallets become things of the past? None of these products has achieved the mass-market

An example of this new form of software customization is the Nokia 6670, targeted at 'prosumers', and the Nokia 7610, targeted at the lifestyle imaging market

success of mobile phones and they remain, from a consumer perspective, in a niche which will gradually disappear due to the emergence of smartphones.

vCard
The vCard standard defines the format of an electronic business card. All devices supporting vCard can exchange information such as phone numbers and addresses. For instance, a user with a vCard-aware phonebook application on a computer can easily transfer names and phone numbers to a vCard-aware mobile phone via Bluetooth, infrared or email.

In the future mobile technology industry, dedicated devices may merge into single devices. Most of us prefer to carry as few devices as possible, and the mobile phone is the one we cannot do without. In future, mobile phone manufacturers will deliver smartphones with features that include:

- more options for connecting your device, driven by 3G, WiMax, WiFi, Bluetooth

- fixed and mobile convergence, driven by VoIP services such as Skype
- music, driven by availability of micro hard disks and flash memory
- imaging, driven by multi-megapixel cameras
- enhanced messaging such as email and instant messaging
- financial transactions, driven by the need for secure transactions
- video streaming and broadcast TV, driven by standards such as DVB-H
- location-based services, driven by GPS chipsets.

In addition to integrating consumer electronics, smartphones could also become embedded in other systems, such as cars. Already, top-of-the range cars include GPS navigation aids; some integrate Bluetooth to enable phone calls on the move. It seems that the limit for the smartphone market opportunity will be limited only by the imagination of manufacturers.

Multimode

A multimode mobile phone works on multiple radio standards. For this to be possible, a phone must have hardware that allows it to process the different signal types. For instance, WCDMA is designed with GSM compatibility in mind, easing the creation of phones that receive both signal types. This is important as it allows the gradual introduction of WCDMA (3G) networks without forcing customers to give up the wide coverage of GSM (2G) networks.

CHAPTER 7

Network Operators

Mobile phones are bigger than any other consumer electronic device in the world. Not literally, of course – the physical size of mobile phones has diminished while the number of phones in circulation has grown beyond the wildest dreams of any analyst. Hundreds of millions of mobile phones ship every year, far exceeding the shipments of comparable consumer devices.

However, the complexity of exploiting this vast market pushes the technical, logistical and financial boundaries of all suppliers involved, not least network operators themselves. The technical, feature and functional requirements coming from network operators continue to expand, and they are ever more complex in terms of development and interoperability requirements. To further complicate the situation, network operators want smartphones that can address niche areas in their portfolios, and they increasingly expect shorter lead times to market.

The competitive landscape of the global mobile phone network operator community is evolving at a tremendous pace. Major network operators across the globe are faced with saturated local markets, intense price competition

Network operator
The term 'network operator' (also referred to as 'operator') applies to a telephone company that provides telecommunication services via a wireless network to a large subscriber base of mobile phone users. Big names among network operators include Vodafone, with about 165 million subscribers around the world; China Mobile with close to 250 million; and China Unicom with around 124 million. But it is not all about subscriber base, and in terms of influence Japan's NTT DoCoMo is a global pioneer in next generation services.

and the commoditization of their core services. It is becoming increasingly difficult to retain customers due to the impact of, amongst other things, competitors' subsidies for mobile phones and the ability for subscribers to retain their phone numbers when switching networks.

Established operators are also facing challenges on new fronts. They are now competing for market share and recognition with mobile virtual network operators (MVNOs), mobile phone vendors, and other new entrants, each trying to attract individual consumers as well as enterprise customers (we look at enterprise in more detail in Chapter 10).

Rank	Company	Technology	Subscribers (in millions)
1	China Mobile	GSM	234.88[2]
2	Vodafone	UMTS, GSM	165.01[3]
3	China Unicom	GSM, CDMA	124.15[2]
4	T-Mobile	UMTS, GSM	80.88[3]
5	América Móvil	GSM, TDMA	73.76[3]
6	Telefónica Móviles	UMTS, GSM, CDMA	69.94[3]
7	Orange	UMTS, GSM	66.74[3]
8	Cingular	UMTS, GSM, TDMA	52.30[2]
9	MTS	GSM	52.21[2]
10	NTT DoCoMo	PDC, FOMA	50.89[2]

The world's largest mobile phone network operators[1]

[1] Source: http://en.wikipedia.org/wiki/List_of_mobile_network_operators
[2] These numbers are correct as at September 2005
[3] These numbers are correct as at June 2005

Mergers, acquisitions, the formation of new industry alliances and internal re-organizations are all recurring themes among the world's largest operators as they chase revenues and greater profitability. These activities are driven by the need to maximize the return on investment in 3G licenses, infrastructure and services and growing or maintaining their average revenue per user.

Challenges facing network operators

Average revenue per user (ARPU) is a fairly self-explanatory measure of the amount of revenue a single subscriber provides to a network. This, and its close relative average profit per user (APPU) are key performance indicators for network operators around the world. Since the beginning of 2000, network-operator revenue based on voice calls per user has been falling. This has been due to several factors, not least that market growth rates have slowed, while price competition between networks has grown. As the mobile market evolves to 3G, with greater network capacity available, they have been attempting to compensate for declining voice revenues by encouraging non-voice services such as multimedia messaging, downloadable ringtones and mobile Internet access.

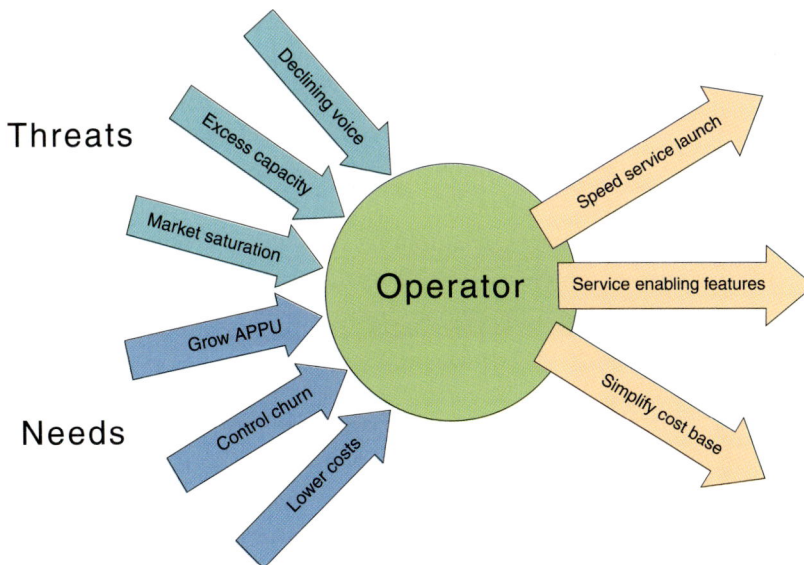

Threats

Declining voice
Excess capacity
Market saturation

Operator

Speed service launch
Service enabling features
Simplify cost base

Needs

Grow APPU
Control churn
Lower costs

Network operators face a multitude of challenges to remain at the forefront of service provision to their subscribers

It is against this dynamic market backdrop that mobile phone network operators are making fundamental strategic choices about the kinds of mobile phones they procure from manufacturers. A few years ago it was rare to see high-end, high-priced phones with built-in cameras, video capability, color screens, stereo sound and other advanced multimedia or enterprise-oriented features. Today, such features have become commonplace in most geographic markets in all but the low-end device categories.

To meet the challenges of addressing customer needs while remaining competitive, network operators are becoming more demanding of their suppliers. Mobile phone manufacturers are required to deliver ever more features at the lowest price and in the shortest timescales. This accelerated development cycle has seen operators wrestling with the task of identifying and launching the 'killer' applications and services that will enable them to make a return on the investment they have made. To add to the complexity of the challenge, they have had to manage a wide variety of mobile phones, based on different operating systems, from multiple vendors on which they need to deliver a consistent customer experience.

The driving need for network operators to control their own destinies and to engage more closely with their customers makes an open operating system extremely attractive. It has also begun to change the dynamics of the mobile phone industry. Where previously mobile phone manufacturers controlled the user experience within a 'closed' environment, increasingly, network operators want to exert control over their end-to-end service offerings, and this includes a desire to obtain more control over the mobile phone itself. Control or 'influence' over a smartphone with an open operating system is critically dependent on the user interface, the point where the mobile phone user engages: firstly with the phone itself and then in some way with the network.

In the operating system arena, the role and requirements of network operators are therefore very important and influential. The introduction of 3G for the masses is a major focus for the network operator community, as the availability of 3G devices in large volumes will not only drive operators to introduce new applications and services, but also presents an opportunity for them to improve and re-position existing services that have yet to achieve significant levels of customer adoption, and drive up their ARPU.

The requirements of network operators

Smartphones based on Symbian OS are sold by mobile phone manufacturers to more than 200 mobile phone network operators worldwide. So why does

Symbian need to engage directly with the network operator community? The answer is that operators are the customers of Symbian's customers (the mobile phone manufacturers) and are, therefore, significant to Symbian's commercial success.

Network operators may be indirect customers, but they play a highly influential role in the Symbian revenue and supply chain. Degrees of influence of network operators and their device strategies can differ significantly, which makes it more important to have a close relationship. For instance, NTT DoCoMo specifies smartphone requirements directly to manufacturers, preferring to keep a tight rein on its customer experience. To generate operator interest and, ultimately, for them to buy Symbian OS smartphones for their portfolios, it is imperative for Symbian to understand the individual requirements of network operators and how they can be met.

Operator device acceptance
Network trials of new mobile phones are the final gateway onto the mobile phone network. If a Symbian OS smartphone fails to meet certain criteria, the device launch will be delayed, or perhaps not even happen! Effectively, device acceptance is the process that ensures stakeholders (chiefly manufacturers and network operators) agree that not only is the time right to launch a certain device, but that it reaches the required standard. Device testing can commonly include three major steps before acceptance: laboratory tests, network testing, and user trials.

Network operators now recognize that the ability to brand and manage the customer experience through a mobile phone is an increasingly powerful tool for service differentiation and revenue growth. Smartphones are inherently capable of being customized, but network operators do not always have the in-house expertise to realize this – by directly engaging with them, Symbian can provide strategic and technical support.

Network operators also have increasing influence over the traditional role of mobile phone manufacturers, as they drive increasingly complex terminal requirements. This makes compliance challenging and costly, so direct engagement enables exchange of product and service requirement and their integration into future releases of Symbian OS. This direct input from the network operators is a valuable contribution to the technology plans developed by Symbian and its licensees.

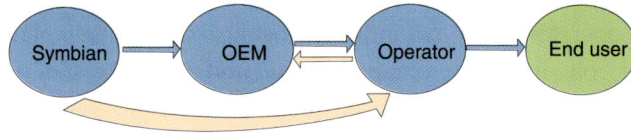

Symbian creates demand for Symbian OS as a platform by engaging with operators in addition to its core customers, mobile phone manufacturers

Symbian engages with the operator community at all levels related to operating system strategy, from marketing, engineering, research and development, and service planning to developer and partner community relations. Generally, the focus of direct engagement activity is on the major network operators in each geographic region (those seen in the operator league table). These are the network operators that have the scale, subscriber base, global reach and resources to make the most positive impact on the smartphone market.

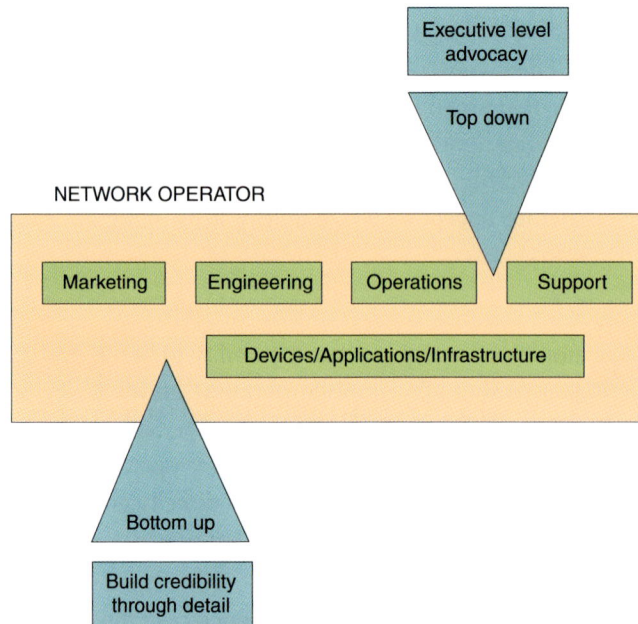

Symbian engages with operators at all levels of the organization, from board-level advocacy to support for developers

Symbian is a participant in the major operators' smartphone requirements processes. These are used as the basis for operator device strategy planning and procurement. To aid strategic alignment of Symbian OS, a strategic global technical forum is facilitated by Symbian and ongoing technical workshops address rapidly evolving areas of technology such as device management, multimedia, digital rights management (DRM), Wireless LAN (WLAN) and security. This also encourages network operator adoption of Symbian-led initiatives that promote the evolution of the smartphone market. An example is the industry-wide support for Symbian Signed (see Chapter 9), which drives industry best practice in third-party application development and certification.

Symbian also collaborates with operators to identify unique device propositions, for example music- or business-centric phones, that address a particular niche in the operator's phone portfolio and which can exploit the capabilities of Symbian OS.

Easing the deployment of new applications is a high priority and Symbian works to ensure that the technologies central to operator commercial service deployment plans are implemented as rapidly as possible on Symbian phones. This is partly achieved through close partner relationships with independent software vendors (ISVs) in the smartphone ecosystem and the operator community to support innovation.

Multiple platforms

Supporting multiple device platforms is becoming an ever greater burden for operators. The practical difficulties of deploying heterogeneous platforms and ensuring these can support, and be supported by the myriad new data-oriented operator service offerings – for example, those associated with gaming, video, messaging, multimedia and TV – is forcing operators to consider a reduction in the number of device platforms.

To address these concerns, many operators are adopting a small number of common infrastructure and device platforms. Increasingly, Symbian OS is being adopted at the heart of this device platformization strategy.

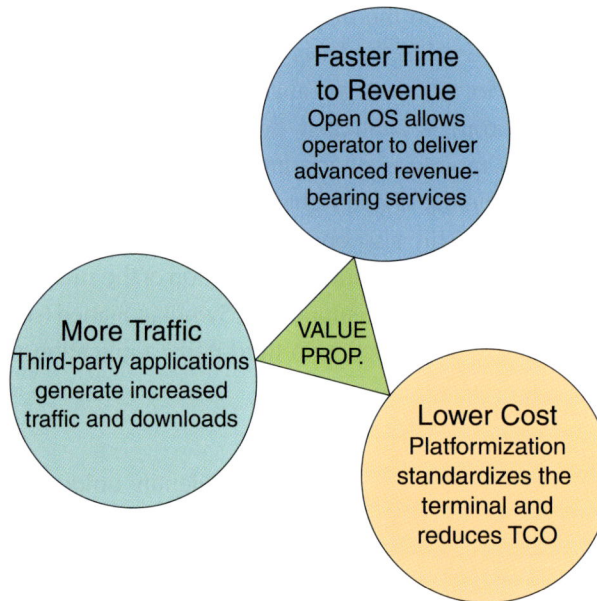

Faster Time to Revenue
Open OS allows operator to deliver advanced revenue-bearing services

More Traffic
Third-party applications generate increased traffic and downloads

VALUE PROP.

Lower Cost
Platformization standardizes the terminal and reduces TCO

Widely deploying a common smartphone platform delivers many benefits to operators

A common deployment platform enables operators to reduce fragmentation and the costs of device procurement, development, infrastructure, interoperability testing and support. It helps to deliver a consistent experience to customers, and it targets resources where they receive maximum return: on differentiating services and content that will enable the operator to generate new revenue streams and attract customers away from the competition.

If this platform is also based on an open operating system, such as Symbian OS, it can reduce the amount of time required to customize a phone – increasingly, operators are demanding unique customization of phones, support for differentiated services, and the ability to convey their own brand and user experience. Basing customization on a common platform introduces efficiency and cost savings, as service creation can also be undertaken by a community of independent developers.

Network operators can also use an open operating system to focus on their core business as a customer service company. In-life costs of smartphones can be reduced through the ability to deliver software patches over the air, ensuring updates can be delivered rapidly to customers when they are needed. Customer care procedures can be simplified by using common device management platforms, reducing the number of platforms in which the customer care department needs to be proficient. It is also possible to launch services across multiple phones from multiple manufacturers without a reliance on specific devices being available at specific times. And finally, it enables the operator to refresh its portfolio of services without expensive replacement of phones, by launching new services to an existing installed base of smartphones.

Understanding market requirements

While network operators are indirect customers of Symbian, they are critical to Symbian's commercial success. Direct engagement is crucial for Symbian to understand the operators' technical and commercial needs and expectations. As mentioned earlier, network operators trial new mobile phones before they allow them onto the network. If a mobile phone fails to meet the standard, its launch could be delayed or even canceled, at a massive cost to all involved.

Typically, a mobile phone enters the market nine to 12 months after Symbian has released the version of Symbian OS on which it is based. To reach the point where Symbian is ready to release a new version, considerable requirements analysis and prioritization will have already been conducted. Symbian can therefore benefit from as much advance notice of operator technical requirements as possible.

There are three main mechanisms by which Symbian obtains operator requirements. These are a high-level strategic forum led by Symbian, expert technical and marketing workshops with individual operators, and by participation in the operators' formal device requirements processes.

Symbian conducts a high-level strategic forum, held approximately three times per year, with a selection of Tier 1 operators from around the world. Members of the forum receive first-hand knowledge of Symbian's product strategy and plans, and can propose specific technology for inclusion in Symbian OS. The forum also presents an opportunity to address common issues amongst operators (for example, platform and application security, and digital rights management).

Expert workshops focus on more technical detail, and are usually conducted on a one-to-one basis with an operator. At these sessions, Symbian and the operator bring together their respective product planning managers and subject matter experts to explore more deeply specific technical topic areas such as SIP, WiFi, digital rights management, device management, security, application certification and Java.

Formal device requirements processes are the foundations of operator device procurement and selection processes. Requirements can run to several hundred detailed pages and provide deep insight into the feature and functionality expectations that the operator has for each device by category. Although many technical requirements are generic, such as the low-level telephony standards defined by the various industry bodies such as the GSM Association (GSMA) and Open Mobile Alliance (OMA), other requirements are bespoke, and if delivered, will put the mobile phone vendor in a strong position with operators when they make their portfolio purchase decisions.

GSMA

The GSM Association (GSMA) is the global trade association that exists to promote, protect and enhance the interests of GSM mobile phone network operators throughout the world. At the end of July 2005, it consisted of 680 second- and third-generation mobile phone network operators and more than 150 manufacturers and suppliers. The Association's members provide mobile phone services to approaching 1.47 billion customers across more than 210 countries and territories around the world. The GSMA aims to accelerate the implementation of collectively identified, commercially prioritized operator requirements and to take leadership in representing the global GSM mobile phone network operator community with one voice on a wide variety of issues nationally, regionally and globally.

GSM is a living and evolving wireless communications standard that already offers an extensive and feature-rich 'family' of voice and data services. The GSM family consists of today's GSM, General Packet Radio Service (GPRS), Enhanced Data rates for GSM Evolution (EDGE) and third-generation GSM services (3GSM) based on the latest WCDMA technology.

GPRS

General Packet Radio Service (GPRS) is a radio technology for GSM networks that adds packet-switching protocols, provides shorter set-up time for ISP connections, and offers the possibility of charging by the amount of data sent rather than connection time. GPRS supports data transmission rates typically up to 20 or 30 Kbps (with a theoretical maximum of 171.2 Kbps), as well as continuous connection to the network. A 2.5G enhancement to GSM, GPRS is a significant step towards 3G, needing a similar business model and service and network architectures (see Chapter 1).

OMA

The Open Mobile Alliance (OMA) was formed in June 2002 by nearly 200 companies including the world's leading mobile phone network operators, device and network suppliers, information technology companies, and content and service providers. The fact that the whole value chain is represented in OMA marks a change in the way specifications for mobile services are created. Rather than keeping the traditional approach of organizing activities around 'technology silos', with different standards and specifications bodies representing different mobile phone technologies, working independently, OMA is aiming to consolidate into one organization all specification activities in the service enabler space.

OMA is the focal point for the development of mobile service enabler specifications, which support the creation of interoperable end-to-end mobile services. OMA drives service enabler architectures and open enabler interfaces that are independent of the underlying wireless networks and platforms. OMA creates interoperable mobile data service enablers that work across devices, service providers, operators, networks, and geographies. Toward that end, OMA will develop test specifications, encourage third-party tool development, and conduct test activities that allow vendors to test their implementations.

In their quest to achieve greater return on investment from their networks and mobile phone investments, the operators are increasingly integrating application requirements into their formal device requirements, again creating a preference for those devices that can support the value-added data services that are critical to future operator revenue streams. This aspect of the requirements is of particular interest to the smartphone industry, as it is the flexible support for these applications that is a unique and differentiating factor for open platforms.

The network operators issue and communicate their formal requirements to mobile phone manufacturers and core technology providers such as Symbian at different times throughout the year. Although this provides an ongoing stream of useful information for analysis and response, it also places ever-increasing pressure on mobile phone manufacturers, due to the sheer volume and growing complexity of the demands.

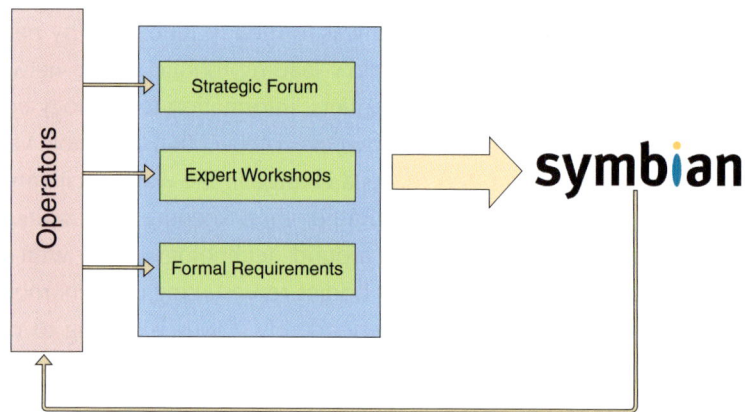

Operator engagement ensures Symbian meets requirements by providing a better product for mobile phone manufacturers

Although not compelled to respond in all cases (remembering that the primary audience for the requirements is the mobile phone manufacturers), Symbian does in fact respond to many network operators requirements documents. Working through this compliance analysis is an extremely detailed process, but it creates the opportunity for Symbian to build relationships with network operators, and provides extensive input for Symbian's own product roadmap development.

Symbian developers

Network operators are an integral part of the Symbian ecosystem and leading operators are Symbian partners and regularly participate in developer activities. Other than the obvious relationship that exists between the device vendors and the operators, there is particular synergy in the areas of developer community activity and commercial partners.

Symbian and many mobile phone manufacturers have an extensive world-wide base of developers writing applications for the platform. Increasingly, operators are looking to implement their own developer programs and foster a developer community to focus on delivering applications that meet their specific market needs. Collaborating on joint developer initiatives around training, access to development tools and reference material, and co-marketing are all important, ongoing activities that bring value to the ecosystem for operator benefit.

Future challenges

The operator landscape continues to evolve. Mergers and acquisitions, together with reorganization within the operators themselves will deliver changes in strategy around device selection and service deployment. However, operator demand for devices offering a given set of functionality at ever reducing price-points, the requirement for longer battery life, the ability to customize in order to deliver the desired user experience with minimum effort, and the ability to support at lower operating costs, will remain.

Symbian OS smartphones are becoming more and more prevalent in operator device portfolios. In the near- to mid-term, competition exists from not only other open platform providers but also the closed proprietary platforms developed by mobile phone manufacturers themselves. The key challenges, and opportunities, for the future are focused on the fundamental changes in network architecture and convergence. The blurring of the boundaries between fixed and mobile networks, terminals and services, and ownership of the customer will present new opportunities for the smartphone industry.

CHAPTER 8

Semiconductor Manufacturers

Symbian OS mobile phones are designed first and foremost to be good telephones, with quality voice calls and excellent battery life. In addition, open Symbian OS smartphones are designed to provide opportunities for interesting and novel software. Achieving these goals requires hardware designed specifically for the task, with high performance for key functionality and an obsession with low power usage.

The design of Symbian OS smartphones typically includes two key domains. The first is a mobile radio interface or baseband processor (BP), which is also known as the modem. This is the part that deals with the wireless telephony, receiving radio signals and converting them to voice. The second

---

Integrated circuit

An integrated circuit (IC) is a thin chip consisting of at least two interconnected semiconductor devices, mainly transistors but also passive components such as resistors. Among the most advanced integrated circuits are microprocessors, which drive everything from computers to digital microwave ovens to mobile phones.

Semiconductor

A semiconductor is a material of which the conductivity can be manipulated, for instance by the addition of impurities, by the introduction of an electric field, by exposure to light, or by other means. A typical semiconducting material is silicon. Semiconductor components are used to create integrated circuits.

domain is an application processor (AP), which runs computational functions such as the user interface and high-level code such as applications. Each of these domains is based on an integrated circuit, commonly referred to as a 'chip'. Surrounding these domains is a collection of peripherals that make up a smartphone: the battery, display, speakers, SIM card and more.

The diagram below shows a 'two-chip solution' in which the baseband processor and the application processor are self-contained systems on separate chips, with a high speed 'inter-processor communication' link between them. This is the most common design for 3G phones, in which each domain can re-use existing software and hardware sub-systems.

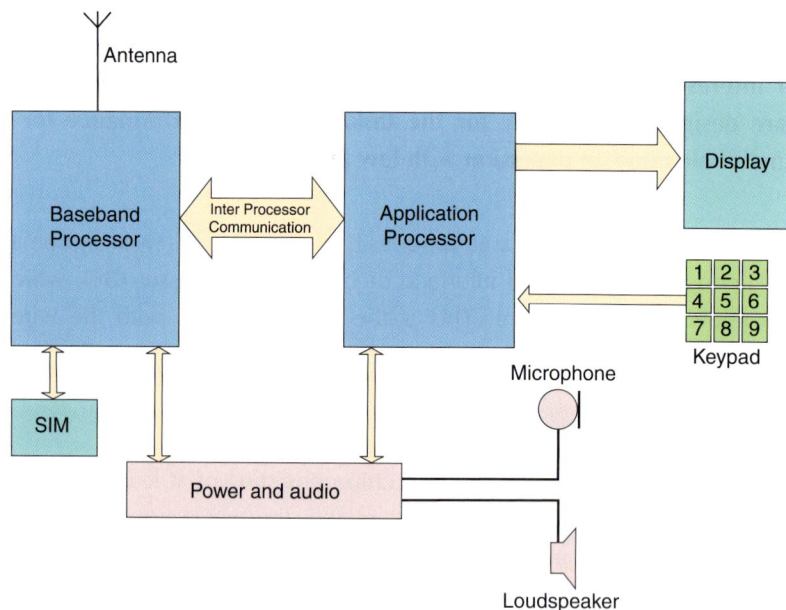

Symbian OS v9 enables mobile phone manufacturers to develop smartphones using a single processor, or chip

Baseband and application processors

The two-domain system of application processor and baseband processor isolates each processor from the other's requirements. The baseband processor requires hard real-time software and periodic power management and provides security between the smartphone and the network. The application processor operates in two modes – full power when a user is interacting with the mobile phone and a deep sleep idle (or 'off mode') when nothing is happening. The application processor contains the frameworks and libraries for built-in applications and third-party code.

The baseband processor

The baseband processor is the voice and data modem for the phone – historically, it was only used for voice processing (converting voice into digital signals) in mobile phones. It contains all the electronics required for the radios used in 2.5G and 3G telephony. It runs the algorithms to decode information, coordinates with the network base stations and communicates with the AP.

The application processor

The application processor is at the heart of a Symbian OS smartphone. Contained on a single piece of silicon, it is an example of a system on a chip (SoC). It normally comprises an ARM processor core, on which Symbian OS runs, along with a number of dedicated hardware engines for improving/accelerating multimedia and 3D graphics performance. It also provides the standard interfaces a phone requires for emerging technologies such as USB, memory cards, and external memory devices (such as Flash, Nand Flash, DRAM and SRAM). This device has traditionally been found in high-end phones that require high-performance audio, video and data capability.

The single-chip solution

Semiconductor companies are now combining the baseband and application processors commonly used today onto a single IC, thereby providing a less costly single-chip product. These can have a single ARM processor core or multiple ARM processor cores depending on the architecture. Better design and manufacturing techniques are allowing this to become both practical and cost effective.

In alignment with this, Symbian introduced a hard real-time kernel in Symbian OS v8.1b that allows manufacturers to build Symbian OS phones based on a single ARM processor core that also hosts the 2.5G

The application processor from a Symbian OS smartphone. For a deeper look inside a smartphone, see Chapter 1

or 3G telephony software. This is enabling lower cost and physically smaller mobile phones to be made that run Symbian OS – driving Symbian OS into the high-volume, mid-tier mobile phone market.

Semiconductor and mobile phone manufacturers

Historically, manufacturers of mobile phones have designed and developed baseband processors and application processors themselves, and engaged with semiconductor companies to manufacture these products specifically for them. However, the cost of producing a smartphone chip is very expensive (development costs running to millions of dollars) and carries the risk that the chip will not meet its original design specifications. In order to cut down this expense, mobile phone manufacturers now deliver their chip specifications to a semiconductor company and allow that company to take on the expense of development.

This is a viable proposition for a semiconductor supplier as it has the opportunity to sell this product to other mobile phone manufacturers and therefore get a better return on a multi-million dollar investment. With this model, mobile phone manufacturers can send the same specification to a number of suppliers and enable a competitive process for best performance and lowest cost products.

Once a chip is manufactured, it is delivered to the mobile phone manufacturer for testing. Testing and debugging a chip is another expensive and risky process. As a result, mobile phone manufacturers insist that some of this validation is also performed by the semiconductor company, so that when they receive the chip it comes ready to use with an evaluation board, software, and test results.

Types of semiconductor company

Traditional semiconductor companies such as Texas Instruments (TI), ARM, Intel, Renesas, ST Microelectronics, Freescale Semiconductor and Samsung Semiconductor have their own manufacturing facilities. These are known as wafer fabrication plants (and are often referred to as 'wafer FAB', or 'Silicon FAB'). The major advantage for these companies of having manufacturing facilities is that they have early access to leading-edge, cost-effective manufacturing processes, providing complete control over process optimization and, as a result, the component costs of the semiconductors they build.

The remaining 'FABless' semiconductor companies (who do not own their own factories) such as Broadcom, Ericsson Mobile Platforms (EMP) and Qualcomm subcontract manufacture of their semiconductor components to silicon foundries such as TSMC, Chartered Semiconductor and UMC. These FABless semiconductor companies tend to offer a more complete system solution to compensate for the slightly higher manufacturing costs that they incur.

Semiconductor companies and Symbian

Symbian delivers Symbian OS source code to semiconductor companies under a development license. They then develop a software interface that allows Symbian OS to work with their semiconductor product.

These hardware-specific software interfaces are known as hardware adaptations (or base ports) and are required for each semiconductor product. There are many semiconductor products available for mobile phone manufacturers to choose from at any one time. The responsibility for hardware adaptation therefore lies with the semiconductor companies, as it would be impossible for Symbian to do a hardware-specific adaptation for each semiconductor product in the market.

The semiconductor company then delivers its semiconductor product and the hardware adaptation software to a mobile phone manufacturer who will customize and optimize it to meet the requirements of a specific smartphone they are developing.

Each major Symbian OS release (Version 8 for example) is developed and validated by Symbian on a single hardware platform only. This hardware platform may change from one major Symbian OS release to the next, depending on the requirements of that release. This is known as Symbian's hardware reference platform (HRP).

Bringing value to smartphones

It is imperative that a semiconductor company works with Symbian during the very early stages of designing their semiconductor products (application processors and baseband processors that include application subsystems). Joint development normally begins at the design concept stage, which can be as much as three or four years before a semiconductor product appears in a smartphone. This close collaboration between Symbian and semiconductor manufacturers ensures that the products they are designing will be compatible with future versions of Symbian OS, and will meet the requirements of the market (which are the requirements of mobile phone manufacturers).

Just one semiconductor product costs millions of dollars to develop and manufacture so it is imperative that they get the design right first time, and find ways to reduce the time from initial product concept through chip design and software development stages to mass production of a smartphone.

By working closely with Symbian (and mobile phone manufacturers) at a very early stage, a semiconductor company ensures that when their semiconductor product becomes available, there is a version of Symbian OS that runs efficiently on it. This hardware/software combination can be taken to any mobile phone manufacturer to win profitable business which will enable the semiconductor company to maximize the return on its investment. For Symbian, working with semiconductor companies at this

Design and development cycle for a new semiconductor product

Year 1:

- ARM Ltd starts development of its latest uProcessor core (for example, ARM 9x/ARM11x).
- Symbian engineering teams and ARM Ltd collaborate to ensure the technology is architecturally compatible with future versions of Symbian OS.

Year 2:

- Lead semiconductor company works with ARM Ltd to manufacture test chips to prove new microprocessor technology works as intended (manufacturing and testing cycle alone can take from five to eight months).
- Semiconductor company starts design and manufacture of its application processor and baseband modem chips (from initial design to availability of first silicon normally takes in the order of 12–18 months).

Year 3:

- Semiconductor company delivers engineering samples of its product, along with Symbian OS and hardware adaptation software, to the mobile phone manufacturer.
- Mobile phone manufacturer starts the mobile phone development cycle, working with the semiconductor company and Symbian to customize hardware and software deliverables and develop a smartphone-specific platform.

Year 3/4:

- Final production version of Symbian OS is delivered to the mobile phone manufacturer.
- Final smartphone (complete with phone-specific hardware including optimized and fully debugged software) is delivered to network operators for field testing and final qualification on their networks (see Chapter 6).
- Mobile phone ships.

early stage (long before a mobile phone manufacturer decides to build a Symbian OS smartphone), ensures its operating system plans are aligned with the semiconductor platforms that mobile phone manufacturers will adopt in the future.

As a major Symbian OS release approaches, Symbian will use a hardware reference platform (HRP) to develop and validate that specific version of Symbian OS. This is to ensure that the Symbian OS version that mobile phone manufacturers receive has been thoroughly tested on real hardware, representative of the hardware that they will build their phones on. This leads to much higher quality software being delivered by Symbian and reduces the development cycle (lowering costs) for the mobile phone manufacturer.

Most of the smartphone ecosystem (those companies developing software, applications, complementary technologies and smartphones) need early access to hardware to develop their technologies. Semiconductor companies provide the 'early access' hardware that allows development of technology to take place in advance of actual smartphone development. It ensures that ecosystem technologies, which are essential to the deployment of Symbian OS, are developed and thoroughly debugged before they are drawn together in a smartphone.

Chips in future

In a short space of time, the market has shifted from semiconductor companies providing a manufacturing service (custom integrated circuits) to them providing standard integrated circuits along with a large amount of software, including test platforms. As the pressure increases from mobile phone manufacturers to further reduce development cost and time-to-market for mobile phones, semiconductor companies will be called upon to supply more complete and optimized hardware and software solutions that are fully validated. Effectively, this will mean producing 'reference designs' – hardware packages with integrated telephony software and a user interface. Just as the assembly line allowed Henry Ford to mass-produce his cars, this approach enables mobile phone manufacturers to quickly build new devices without high one-off development costs.

This is natural evolution in a consumer electronics market, and has already happened in the low end of the phone market (voice-only phones). Many semiconductor companies now supply reference designs based on their 2G/2.5G (GSM/GPRS) silicon platforms to mobile phone manufacturers. The accelerating adoption of Symbian OS and migration to 3G means that the expense of maintaining and growing market share will be greater for semiconductor companies, and those that embrace the move to reference designs will be the eventual winners in this emerging market.

CHAPTER 9

The Symbian Developer

Symbian OS developers are individuals or groups of individuals who extend the capabilities of Symbian OS by creating applications that run on and utilize the technology of Symbian OS-based phones. Developers exist at every level of the Symbian ecosystem, from hobbyists who write code for pleasure and admire the design and possibilities of Symbian OS, to large developer teams within mobile phone manufacturers who create a range of Symbian OS applications and games in order to enhance the consumer appeal of the mobile phones they produce. Developers are the development teams and partners of network operators; they are the IT managers that integrate the enterprise applications into the mobile phones of company executives; they are the teams that integrate Symbian OS into new hardware; and they are the developers that bring their innovations to Symbian OS phones from other platforms like Java. They are the engine of the smartphone economy.

Symbian is an open platform and thus allows applications to be developed and added to Symbian OS mobile phones. Being an open platform gives Symbian OS developers the potential for a huge amount of choice and innovation. By Q3 2005, there were over 5000 different applications recorded as being available for Symbian OS and the number of application releases is growing at an average of around 20% per quarter, illustrating the strength of the smartphone economy. These are compelling reasons to develop for Symbian OS. Mobile software development of the past has focused on more traditional PDA-style devices. With these, entire product lines sold in the order of around 10 or 20 million over their entire lifespan. In contrast, smartphones offer the potential for developers to reach hundreds of millions of consumers. As Symbian continues to successfully ship Symbian OS in increasing numbers of smartphones, which in turn reach more mass-market segments, the opportunities for developers are also increasing.

Good developers also appreciate technical elegance – and Symbian OS offers this throughout. Part I of this book discussed the many clever and unique features that were designed into Symbian OS to ensure it is robust and reliable. Working with Symbian OS allows developers to create many technically appealing solutions, fostering good design principles for a best-in-class mobile experience.

The importance of developers

Developers deal with Symbian OS technology day-in–day-out, whether they are developing the operating system itself, integrating technologies to create a specific product (such as the user interface), or designing new applications with which users can customize their smartphone. More than any other stakeholders, they are intimately affected by developments of Symbian OS. The smartphone economy's 'virtuous cycle' is driven by these individuals:

- Developers create the functionality that makes an open platform valuable.
- Collectively, developers form organizations (for example, independent software vendors (ISVs), open source projects, or multinational companies) creating compelling applications and content.
- Developers typically drive innovation and disruption, especially at the grass-roots level.

Compare the following diagram with the virtuous cycle in the introduction to Part II. The 'virtuous cycle' of the developer ecosystem below shows how developers are in fact the engine of the smartphone ecosystem, driving value through innovation in each phase of smartphone and market development.

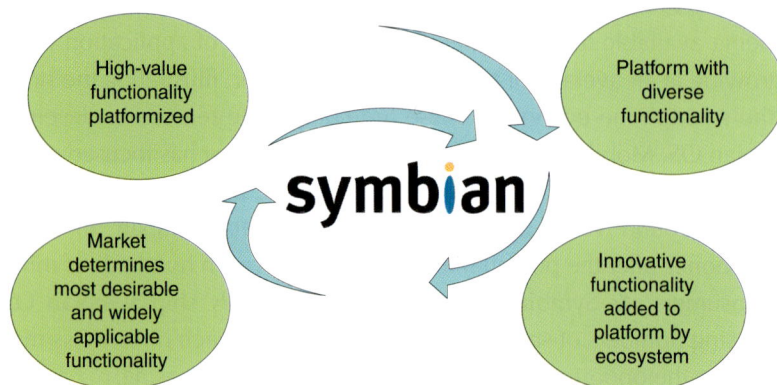

The lifecycle of platform growth and the value of developers

As mobile phone manufacturers ship large volumes of open Symbian OS phones, network operators are able to derive greater revenue by developing new network services that these smartphones can exploit. ISVs engage in this new opportunity by delivering innovative solutions which serve new consumer and business needs. Consumers and enterprises then begin to actively adopt such products and drive demand for open mobile phones which can help them to be more productive.

And so the cycle perpetuates – enhanced by developers not only creating new solutions, but also developing the new integrated network technology which provides the ability to deliver new services which further drive revenue for network operators and in turn adoption from users. Soon all members of the ecosystem are demanding powerful open mobile phones. A virtuous cycle is established where everyone benefits as the market grows.

The primary value of the smartphone ecosystem is the ability for just-in-time customization, personalization and segmentation. At each stage in the value chain, some level of functionality is delivered to the end user by a Symbian developer, whether it is core operating system functionality, UI functionality, on-device customization, in-box differentiation and segmentation, network operator or content provider differentiation, or enterprise or retail applications and content.

> **Content provider**
> A content provider is a company that provides services to mobile phone users or network operators. These services could be shopping, web surfing, chat rooms, playing games, or accessing data such as music and books through a server.

Selling applications

When a product is complete, its developers want to make money from it. This means finding a way to get it to users who will buy it, or making deals with network operators or phone manufacturers that wish to resell it. There are several models that developers use to achieve this, depending on where they focus their development effort and, to a large extent, on the nature of their products and their relationships within the smartphone market.

How a product reaches market depends in many ways on the product itself. Network operators tend to target new applications that use their network and create revenue because users can be billed, for instance, for the time they use downloading information. If an application has particular potential to use the network, it may end up being integrated into a smartphone by the mobile phone manufacturer (often referred to as an 'out-of-the-box' solution, because it is installed before you buy the smartphone). This is particularly attractive, as it guarantees the developer an immediate return in royalties. If these routes to selling a product are not available, then online resellers (such as Handango) enable consumers to find an application and download it to their smartphones. With a multitude of opportunities for new applications to reach consumers, innovations can appear as if from nowhere and change the market very quickly.

Signing applications

While an open platform creates huge advantages for Symbian developers, it is also possible for poorly written third-party software to cause a poor user experience. Symbian has been able to work with industry-leaders to define a common baseline testing and certification program for applications and content, *Symbian Signed*.

Applications which pass the industry-agreed and endorsed testing process are distributed in an exclusive catalog to mobile phone manufacturers and network operators. ISVs also have the right to use the 'for Symbian OS' logo with their products, advertising the fact they have passed the Symbian Signed process and building confidence in their products. More details about this industry-wide program can be found at www.symbiansigned.com.

If your application is signed, it is approved for use anywhere

Symbian also cooperates with leading software retailers to help developers deliver their software to mobile phone users. Partners already benefit from closer alignment and networking opportunities, not just with each other, but also with licensees and network operators, but all ISVs can benefit from the extra exposure and confidence of having their application Symbian Signed, providing network operators with a quality guarantee and reducing deployment risks.

WorldMate by MobiMate

WorldMate is a travel and business application for smartphones that has hundreds of thousands of users worldwide. Its key features include concurrent world clocks with automatic Daylight Savings Time calculation, a world map with day/night display, five-day worldwide weather forecasts from The Weather Channel which integrate with the always-on nature of Symbian OS phones to provide live online updates, a currency converter with daily exchange rate updates, and more. A Professional Edition adds critical travel services such as Flight Schedules (from OAG WorldWide), itinerary management and other advanced features.

Following the successful release of WorldMate for the Sony Ericsson P800 (using the UIQ user interface) in March 2003, the product was generating 90% of MobiMate's sales a year later. Nadav Gur, CEO of MobiMate commented, "The openness and flexibility of Symbian OS allows us to develop and sell great applications, and add value to Symbian OS-based smartphones. Symbian's business model is structured in a way that companies such as ours can make money from the ecosystem that has rapidly grown up around their operating system, and we are delighted to be working so successfully within it."

The product has now been successfully deployed on all major open Symbian OS UI platforms – another example of how Symbian OS allows developers to easily and rapidly target many different types of phone and market segments.

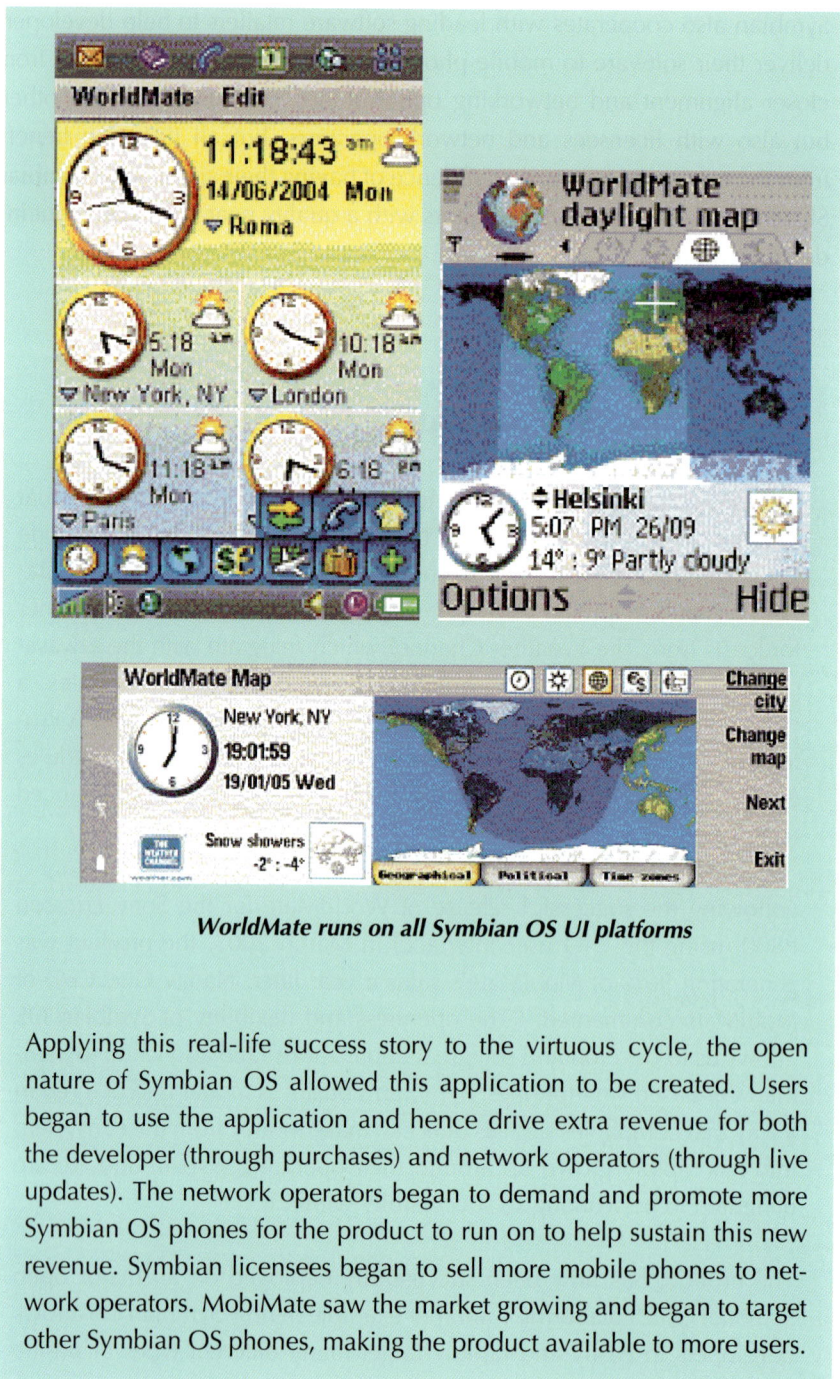

WorldMate runs on all Symbian OS UI platforms

Applying this real-life success story to the virtuous cycle, the open nature of Symbian OS allowed this application to be created. Users began to use the application and hence drive extra revenue for both the developer (through purchases) and network operators (through live updates). The network operators began to demand and promote more Symbian OS phones for the product to run on to help sustain this new revenue. Symbian licensees began to sell more mobile phones to network operators. MobiMate saw the market growing and began to target other Symbian OS phones, making the product available to more users.

Supporting Symbian developers

Symbian OS is an extremely powerful operating system with very advanced functionality. It comprises many millions of lines of source code. From a developer's point of view, this means there are hundreds of functions and features (APIs, see Chapter 4) which they can use in their own applications. Symbian aims to provide a complete end-to-end development experience to make developing for Symbian OS as easy as possible. However, as with the development and evolution of Symbian OS itself, Symbian is not always best-placed to be all things to all people, or to deliver everything itself. As a result, strong cooperation and partnership also exists throughout the developer ecosystem. Let's examine how the Symbian ecosystem helps address the needs of developers.

Development language

Symbian OS itself is developed in the language called C++. As a result, any developer who knows C++ can also write applications for Symbian OS. However, there are many other popular languages available too. Symbian offers developers incredible choice and flexibility between many market-leading and standard development languages, to suit a range of needs and previous experience. To ensure greater choice, Symbian and Sun have brought market-leading Java support to the Symbian OS. Likewise, Microsoft Visual Basic is a popular and easy-to-use language that has been delivered by AppForge, with its 'Crossfire' product for Symbian OS, allowing Microsoft Visual Basic developers to easily port their applications. More detail on these languages is available in Chapter 11.

Software development kits

As the creator of the underlying Symbian OS code, Symbian provides documentation and support for it. Symbian also works closely with the owners of the major UI platforms to ensure they provide software development kits (SDKs) for their platform which incorporate the latest generic Symbian OS APIs and supporting material. There are various kits available for Symbian OS UIs that are developed by mobile phone manufacturers or UI vendors. Although large parts of the underlying Symbian OS code remains the same between the different UI platforms, the layer on top which constitutes the actual UI differs. There are therefore different SDKs to help developers accurately target these platforms. Developers wishing to target more than one platform can run multiple SDKs at the same time.

Tools

Symbian OS development typically begins and mainly takes place on a PC. When it is written, most software code is simply plain text – much like the page you are reading now, but in a different language. To get this code into a language that the lower-level hardware of a mobile phone can actually recognize as a program, it must pass through a compiler which translates the code into a language the hardware understands. Developing a compiler which produces fast and compact code is an entire business in itself – Symbian works with partners such as ARM and Nokia's Tools division (formerly Metrowerks) to ensure good tools are available for developers.

Although it may sound strange to develop mobile phone software on a PC, the reason that this is possible is that all SDKs include a comprehensive 'emulator' for an unbranded, generic Symbian OS user interface. The tools available on PCs to develop and debug software are extremely powerful and cost-effective. Development and initial testing and debugging is carried out on the PC, before the software is installed on a real phone to test its behavior on an actual device and debug any remaining problems. This is, in fact, exactly how Symbian OS itself is developed too – on the emulator first, then on real hardware.

Knowledge

The main portal for all Symbian developers is the 'Symbian Developer Network' portal at **www.symbian.com/developer**. This is where Symbian makes available as much information as possible to help developers produce their applications, including additional tools, example code, technical papers and example projects and knowledge bases. In addition, the Symbian Developer Network is home to some of the liveliest discussion and support forums available relating to Symbian OS development – employees of Symbian, mobile phone manufacturers and partners all participate.

SDKs include a comprehensive set of documents called the 'Symbian OS Library for Application Developers'. This is produced by Symbian to describe what each of the thousands of APIs is meant to do, as well as to provide example code for how a developer can use it in their own code. Knowledge, however, does not just begin and end with the reference material – books, technical training and knowledge bases all help provide vital resources for developers too. Symbian Press publishes material by many Symbian experts to deliver a range of books, aimed both at beginners and at advanced

Symbian developers. These books are an invaluable resource to developers. More details about the series are at the beginning of this book.

Symbian Technical Training is responsible for running tailored courses and 'boot camps' to impart necessary knowledge to developers as quickly as possible. Existing training materials are now being supplemented with a developer certification and recognized accreditation scheme, which will allow developers to prove their competency and further increase the value of Symbian OS development expertise as a recognized, transferable skill. Symbian Partner initiatives extend access to Symbian technology, support and plans to key companies in the developer ecosystem. They also bring members commercial and technical benefits. For example, partners can access the Partner Support Helpdesk and – under guaranteed service level agreements – receive technical support and advice directly from experienced Symbian engineers and experts.

Partners also benefit from greater exposure to Symbian OS licensees and major network operators, helping improve their access to markets for their finished products. Finally, a small number of partners such as Texas Instruments and Intel offer hardware to licensees, from which they build phones. For these partners in particular, privileged access to Symbian's source code and intellectual property helps them not only reduce their time to market (they get to work with new versions of Symbian OS as they are being developed), but also increases their product quality by enabling them to examine and debug their code with source code for reference. Symbian therefore offers its trusted partners the option to license a special development kit which contains additional source and tools (see Chapter 4 for more details).

Success in the smartphone market

Two of Symbian's major 'route to market' partners are Handango (www.handango.com) and Motricity (www.symbiangear.com). Both partners offer a secure, reliable infrastructure through which end users can purchase additional software for their mobile phones.

In March 2005, Handango's market update highlighted the fact that three out of the top five phones most popular for adding new software were powered by Symbian OS. Each of these three phones was based on a different UI platform: the Nokia 9500 (based on Series 80), the Nokia 6680 (based on S60) and the Sony Ericsson P910i (based on UIQ), the last of which was the most popular overall.

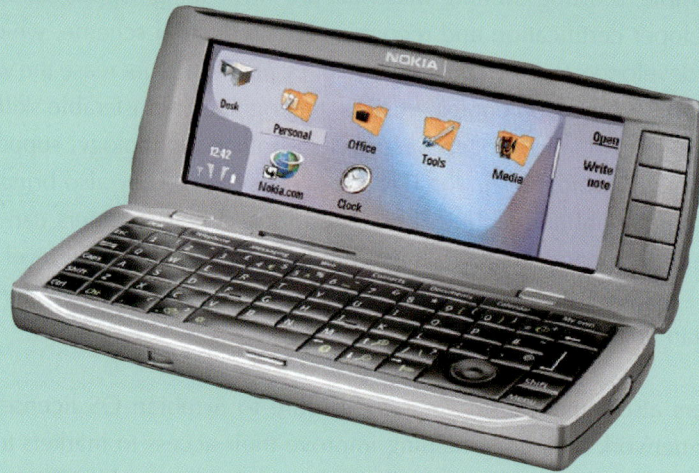

The most popular Symbian OS phones for add-on software

It is a strong endorsement of Symbian OS as a flexible platform that can be used to target a variety of different styles of mobile phone, and indicates that developers are already making substantial sales and generating revenues.

Future development

The challenges for the future are all about coping with growth – Symbian will ensure Symbian OS is the easiest mobile phone platform to develop software for. The huge opportunities which exist for developers thanks to the virtuous cycle are proven and many developers have entered, and are entering, the market. But at the same time, Symbian's technology can result in a steep learning curve for new developers. The coding 'idioms' Symbian employs to ensure that developers produce consistent, robust and reliable code need to be explained and learned. The future for Symbian developers includes:

- better, cheaper – and free – development tools
- support for more standard C++ to make it easier for developers to use code from other platforms on Symbian OS platforms
- improved and extended documentation, training and community activity
- earlier access to new technology to help reduce time to market.

Symbian invests in the ecosystem to ensure the virtuous cycle grows stronger and continues to benefit everyone. Just as Symbian OS smartphones are being used by a wider range of consumers, so Symbian will make Symbian OS easier to develop on, for a wider range of developers.

CHAPTER **10**

Symbian OS for Businesses

Staying connected with colleagues and customers throughout the day is an advantage to any business and its executives. In addition to voice and SMS, smartphones enable a range of opportunities for useful business communication, such as voice conferencing, push-to-talk and connection to corporate server systems to enable access to stored data or information processing (for example, filing expenses while on the move).

Push-to-talk

Push-to-talk (PTT) allows a mobile phone to function as a digital two-way radio. Only one person at a time can talk and one or several others can listen instantly. The service connects mobile phone users with each other within seconds. Currently, PTT users have to belong to the same network in order to talk to one another. PTT commonly does not use up the airtime minutes that are available for general voice calls: it uses a GPRS connection, on which the amount of data transmitted is billed, and not the amount of time a conversation takes. The obvious benefit of this is that calls are cheaper.

The benefit of Symbian OS for an enterprise begins with the functionality on the smartphone that enable individuals to get more done in the day with greater efficiency. Mobile professionals can access their contacts and calendar, synchronize with their desktop PC, and send and receive email using built-in email applications. This is particularly useful for small- to medium-sized businesses accessing ISP-based email or IMAP-enabled Microsoft Exchange servers. This built-in functionality can be enhanced with commercially available applications, such as WorldMate, which equips the business traveler with a world clock, up-to-date weather in various destinations, flight schedules and other handy functionality to help them at their destination.

WorldMate equips the traveler with updated flight, weather and currency information direct to a smartphone

At the next level, there are business process improvements that can be gained by using smartphones. Many of today's business tools are Internet based and all Symbian OS smartphones have the capability to connect to the Internet, and so to exchange data and then work with that data – even when connectivity is intermittent. For example, common business information reporting tools such as Business Objects can be accessed using the built-in web browser, enabling the mobile professional to access information, such as revenue by region and sales margins, on the go.

Enterprises can also enjoy cost savings by using smartphones as a platform for deploying corporate productivity applications. Because Symbian OS supports industry standards and each phone has the same built-in core data communication functionality, IT managers can expect to use the same email gateways and management and support systems for all their Symbian OS smartphones, irrespective of manufacturer.

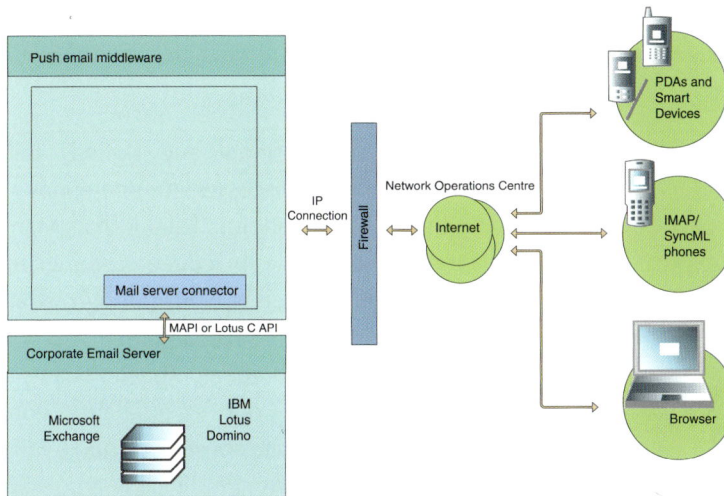

Comprehensive functionality and support for standards means an infrastructure such as the Visto Mobile Enterprise Server can support the user's phone of choice

Mobile services, driven by business needs, drive the adoption of advanced smartphones. Support for standards is critical to this adoption and, as we saw in Part I, every Symbian OS smartphone supports Internet standards. With the technology in place to support the enterprise, Symbian OS and the ecosystem enables businesses to drive the creation of new services without concern for the underlying technology. Enterprise applications on Symbian OS created to meet business needs tend to excel in terms of user experience.

Experience has shown that 'closed' phones or PDAs with browser or single-purpose applications have failed to meet the needs of businesses. More often that not, this is because enterprise requirements have not been fully identified during the planning of mobile phones, or at least not until the pilot stages of a project. On a mobile phone without an open operating system, new applications cannot be added to the finished device and so additional requirements cannot be addressed until a new device is designed and released. This further reinforces the value of an extensible software platform, such as Symbian OS, that is capable of supporting additional application development.

Case Study: Airinmar and Intellisync

Airinmar's aim is to reduce the cost of aircraft component ownership. The company has its headquarters in the UK with direct operations in Hong Kong, Sydney and Miami and has a growing global customer base that includes Qantas, Cathay Pacific, Lufthansa, Air France and Virgin.

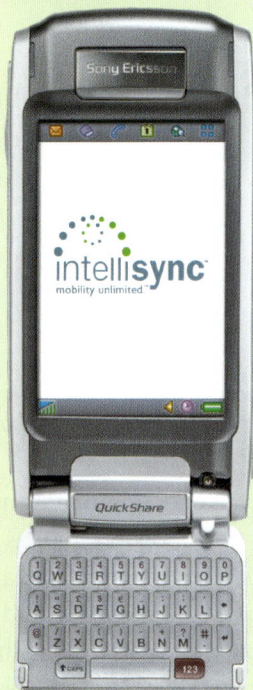

A P910 with a version of Intellisync

Through professional and skilled facilities management processes the company provides a framework for 'Total Repair Management' and is able to reduce customer repair and maintenance spend through strategic sourcing, 'should-cost analysis' and value-engineering techniques. The company does not hold stock nor manufacture components – it negotiates best price and availability from third-party suppliers for its customers. It's an industry that relies heavily on information, everything from sales information, fault-reporting documents, and component spreadsheets to invoicing information. Timely response is vital to success.

With key personnel spending more and more time away from their desks it was becoming increasingly difficult to maintain competitive advantage. To meet – and hopefully exceed – customer expectations, Airinmar decided to implement a smartphone email system.

Airinmar sought the assistance of a system integrator, Handheld PCs. Like Airinmar, Handheld PCs was independent of device manufacturers and network operators, and it was seen as a good match to Airinmar's requirements.

Handheld PCs supplied Sony Ericsson P910s pre-configured with Intellisync Mobile Suite, a complete push email solution with address book and calendar synchronization capabilities. Pre-configuration made deployment easy – a simple case of entering the user PIN number and allowing the smartphone to initialize its synchronization with the corporate email system.

Within minutes, hundreds of contacts, tasks and calendar engagements were downloaded and Airinmar's executives became fully mobile.

The enterprise ecosystem and Symbian

Mobile business needs are being met both by traditional suppliers and by new entrants who are introducing new innovations by exploiting the possibilities enabled by smartphone technology. A good example of the latter is 'push email': every Symbian OS phone can access corporate email and many business users have increased their productivity by using push email solutions, which send an email to a phone as soon as it arrives at the corporate email server.

Push and pull

Email can either be 'pushed' or 'pulled' to a smartphone. The difference between these two methods is intuitive. If a smartphone 'pulls' email, email is only sent to the smartphone from the server when the smartphone requests it. If email is 'pushed' to the smartphone, the server sends email to the smartphone as and when it arrives at the server. The benefit of push email is that the intended recipient will receive it immediately and automatically. The most obvious example of a push email solution is RIM's Blackberry Connect, which is available on Symbian OS phones.

Symbian partners such as Visto, RIM, Seven and Intellisync have created push email solutions for Symbian OS that offer secure, efficient connection to Microsoft Exchange, Lotus Notes and other mainstream email systems.

The self-employed and smaller businesses often have a high dependency on mobile phones to maintain service levels for their customers. These groups drive the uptake of 'productivity applications' such as world clocks, word processor document viewers and expense trackers. Productivity applications usually do not require infrastructure to be installed within the enterprise (such as servers), and since there is a strong crossover with the broader mobile phone consumer segment, these applications can be sold through mainstream online retail channels such as Handango and Motricity (see Chapter 9).

Middleware

Leading software vendors have deployed their middleware onto Symbian OS smartphones. For example, IBM has enabled a new range of applications for both existing and new IBM customers with its WebSphere product. WebSphere has been specially designed for mobile platforms and uses whatever connection is available, whether 2.5G, 3G or WLAN, to connect mobile phones to IBM infrastructure in a business.

Middleware

Middleware is a set of software building blocks which application developers can use to build business applications. Middleware vendors ensure that their middleware takes full advantage of the mobile technology and then expose that functionality in a way that is familiar to application developers. Examples of middleware vendors include IBM with Websphere and Extended Systems with OneBridge.

An important aspect of middleware is that it enables other software vendors to produce line of business applications. Line of business applications relate to areas such as order fulfillment and warehouse stock control where it is very straightforward to evaluate whether a process improvement works or not and which can be measured in the bottom line. For this reason, line of business applications are important to system integrators, as a compelling return on investment case can be made to justify a technology investment. For example, the deployment of a manufacturing stock control application that enables real-time, in-the-field updates can result in huge cost savings. Symbian's engagement with middleware vendors, in turn, enables an ecosystem of organizations that build these applications.

Case Study: TNT and IBM WebSphere

TNT, a global provider of mail, express and logistics, chose to improve efficiency and save costs by using IBM WebSphere. It chose to deploy Nokia 9500s to enable executives to stay abreast of their messages and schedules throughout the day.

TNT was already using IBM infrastructure so the availability of WebSphere on the Nokia 9500 meant they could easily extend email and Sametime (the Lotus Notes version of Instant Messaging) to smartphones.

TNT is also exploring the benefits that mobile phone technology can bring to parcel tracking. Using the Nokia 9500's built-in camera it is possible to capture images of parcel tracking barcodes. The barcode images can be processed on the device and the parcel identification information can be sent immediately (using the 2.5G network) to update TNT's central database with the parcel's location at that time.

Additionally, TNT had an investment in BlackBerry mobile email infrastructure and, rather than carry multiple devices, TNT senior managers preferred to access the BlackBerry on the 9500. They could do this by installing the BlackBerry Connect client that gave them full compatibility with the BlackBerry infrastructure and of course the ability to get email, contacts and calendar information 'pushed' to their 9500s.

Bridging the fixed–mobile divide

Fixed-line telephone service vendors are also bringing their expertise to mobile integration. Integrating the mobile phone with the office phone system (commonly known as Private Branch Exchange, or PBX) makes it easier to contact employees on a single number and allows PBX vendors to increase customer usage of their systems without additional hardware cost. The most-used PBX features can be extended to the smartphone, including call transfer, call parking, pickup, hold, call-back, whisper, conference, drop, forward, send all calls and exclusion. This dramatically increases the business capability of the mobile phone and as a result, the service levels that a business can supply to their customers.

Businesses can also make cost savings by routing international calls via their PBX to take advantage of the competition between long-distance carriers in the fixed-line world. Network operators also benefit from this, winning voice traffic revenues where calls would otherwise have gone to the office voicemail system.

VoIP

Voice over Internet Protocol (VoIP, sometimes pronounced 'voyp') is the transmission of analog voice traffic over digital packet-based networks. The Internet protocol (IP) was originally designed for data networking. The success of IP in becoming a world standard for data networking has led to its adaptation to voice networking.

The practical upshot of this is that by using the VoIP software that is available to make Internet phone calls, users may bypass phone companies (and their charges) entirely.

Deploying the mobile enterprise

In the IT world, system integrators are the organizations that plan, procure, deploy and support large solutions. These same organizations now include in their portfolios the ability to extend business voice and data to mobile systems and provide a business with integrated fixed–mobile solutions.

There are alternatives to the system integrator model, as mobile operators and other retailers introduce various pricing models driven by their ability to bundle hardware, such as laptops, datacards and phones, and support these offers via their predictable voice-plus-data revenue stream.

For those businesses that do not have the scale, expertise or time to investigate the right mobile enterprise solution for their needs, smart-phones can supply the solution in the form of a hosted service. With a hosted service, a network operator establishes a secure connection to the business's IT system and then manages the whole interaction with the phone.

Mobile enterprise challenges

When faced with technology that affects both the company servers and mobile devices, often IT managers will ask for something that 'just works'. What they are asking for is an 'end-to-end' solution which promises to deliver technology that does what it needs to at every part of the system, and so provides the appropriate business benefits. Although the IT industry in general is mature, mobile technology introduces new challenges in areas such as IT infrastructure, data security and which solution to choose. Many of these technical challenges have been solved by Symbian's partners, ensuring that end-to-end solutions for businesses are readily available.

There are three ways in which mobile solution deployment is becoming easier for the business: system integrators, with specialist mobile expertise, are guiding businesses through the process; network operators offering hosted solutions are transferring implementation costs from the enterprise; and consolidation amongst solutions providers is producing comprehensive 'super solutions' that address the key business issues.

Standards organizations and Symbian take the long-term view: the most important objective is to work towards simplified and interoperable solutions. As a consequence, consolidation is occurring and clear market leaders and deployment best practice are emerging as a result. With push email, for example, there are many vendors, many proprietary standards and many channels for deployment. Every IT manager wants to avoid being locked in to a proprietary solution (although this is counterbalanced by early market demands for 'solutions that just work').

Developing the mobile enterprise

The Symbian Enterprise Alliance Council (SEAC) is a forum for Symbian OS phone manufacturers and Symbian Partners who actively target the enterprise segment. The purpose of the forum is to communicate and discuss Symbian's enterprise products and go-to-market strategy.

As end-to-end enterprise solutions are delivered closely in conjunction with partners and network operators, they are an integral part of the forum and have the opportunity to share their market view and set out their expectations. SEAC is an effective way for Symbian to test its enterprise plan and get industry feedback.

In a developing market such as mobile enterprise, real success stories validate corporate investment, and SEAC regularly involves briefings from network operators and pioneering partners to highlight successes and identify new joint opportunities. For instance, the industry is responding to the occasional availability of free bandwidth in the office. Wireless access points can be used to route both voice and data traffic effectively, at no cost.

Now, when a business user wants to check email on their phone in an office meeting room, their smartphone can select a wireless connection. If the user then leaves the office, but wants to maintain the email session, the smartphone will automatically switch to the public 2.5G/3G network. Network operators are beginning to balance the competitive threats of WLAN with the overall business benefits it provides to the end user. Competitive and transparent pricing will triumph in the end.

CHAPTER 11

Java and Other Runtime Frameworks

Throughout this book we have looked at how Symbian provides a development platform: a platform to develop smartphones, a platform to develop user interfaces, and a platform to deploy native (Symbian OS C++) applications and services. In this final chapter, we will look at how Symbian enables other developer platforms – and their developer communities – so that they too can benefit from the opportunities created by a mass market for smartphones.

Support for runtime frameworks is a vital part of Symbian OS. It ensures that Symbian OS appeals to the developer community that does not program using Symbian OS C++ and means that these developers value Symbian OS as an environment that enables them to develop new functionality. Symbian's primary role is to enable the functionality that is created by developers.

In this chapter we will mainly focus on Java, which is ubiquitous on mobile phones. It boasts an installed base in excess of 700 million phones and around four million developers worldwide. Symbian has a long history of support for Java with an implementation available since the first Symbian OS mobile phone was shipped. So what is Java? And why is this runtime system so strategically important to Symbian and the smartphone market?

> **Runtime frameworks**
> A runtime framework is a framework that sits on top of an operating system, such as Symbian OS, and provides the support and resources necessary for a certain type of program to execute. A Java Virtual Machine is an instance of such a runtime framework, allowing Java applications to run on a variety of operating systems.

Java

Java is a modern, general-purpose programming language, developed by Sun Microsystems, which was first released in 1996. It rapidly gathered a huge following, its popularity partly driven by the burgeoning Internet, for which Java technology proved particularly suited to delivering applications. Java made it possible to download applications over the Internet and run them on a local machine (the host). Its popularity as an Internet programming language is a result of several strengths in the Java programming language design and architecture. Principal among these design strengths are security, platform independence and standardization.

Java and platform independence

Computer programs are written in a pseudo-natural language text known as source code (which is easy for – some – people to write and comprehend). To produce code that can actually execute itself on a computer most languages are then compiled into machine code (a set of instructions understood by a processor). The machine code is specific to a processor or, more usually, a processor architecture such as Intel or ARM. Although source code is not specific to a particular processor, in most programming languages (C++, for example) the source code is specific to a particular operating system, since to do anything useful it relies on specific operating system calls known as APIs. These APIs vary from Unix to Windows to Symbian OS, for example.

Source code in itself is not very useful for delivering applications to the end user since it is not in an executable format. So to create an executable to run on different platforms (for example Windows/Intel or Symbian/ARM) not only requires compiling source code into different machine code versions, but also modifying the source code for the particular operating system, a considerable inconvenience to the programmer. Java neatly avoids these issues.

Although Java source code needs to be compiled into an executable format, this format (known as byte code) is platform independent. In other words it will run just as well on Symbian OS/ARM as on Windows/Intel. This platform neutrality is achieved by executing the byte code in what is known as a virtual machine (the Java Virtual Machine or JVM). The JVM provides an intermediate interpreter, translating platform-independent byte code into platform-specific machine code.

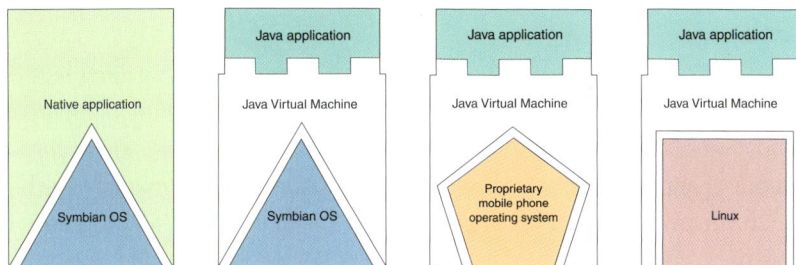

The Java Virtual Machine is customized for each type of operating system so that applications do not need to be

Java and standards

The virtual machine approach adopted by Java also comes to the rescue in terms of source-code independence. In most programming languages, for instance C++, even the source code is specific to the host operating system. This generally means the developer has to rewrite their application's source code when porting the application from Windows to Unix, for example. In the case of Java, the virtual machine enables Java to define a standard API set, which the Java Virtual Machine then translates into the appropriate API calls for the host operating system. This means that not only is the executable byte code platform-neutral, but so also is the source code, enabling the developer to write the application once and run it anywhere. The standard API set is derived through an open process, known as the Java Community Process (JCP) in which any stakeholder can participate, with each API specification known as a Java Specification Request (JSR). Symbian has long been an active participant in the JCP process, helping to define Java in the mobile phone world.

Java and security

The integrity of a host machine executing a Java application must be protected from accidental corruption or malicious attack, thereby ensuring that the user can have confidence that the executing application is well behaved. Java includes a number of built-in security features including the sandbox security model that ensures applications run in a constrained environment with only limited access to the set of functionality available on the host. This prevents rogue Java applications from, for instance, searching the file system of the host machine for credit card details and transmitting them to a remote computer for nefarious purposes.

Evolution of Java

The platform neutrality provided by the Java programming language and the JVM does come at a cost. The intermediate translation of byte code to machine code provided by the virtual machine occurs at runtime (as the application executes). This extra step incurs a performance overhead, which means that Java programs do not execute as fast as programs that have been compiled directly to machine code and can execute directly (like Symbian OS C++). Also, for a Java application (delivered in byte code) to execute, it is necessary for a Java Virtual Machine to be installed on the host machine.

Even so, the strengths of Java such as security and platform independence are generally acknowledged to outweigh its drawbacks, leading to huge popularity with developers. Web browser suppliers soon recognized the strength of Java, incorporating Java Virtual Machines in popular browsers such as Netscape Navigator and Internet Explorer, thus allowing small Java applications (applets) to be downloaded over the web and run within these browsers.

Coinciding with the huge growth of the Internet, the versatility of these Java applets boosted the popularity and take up of Java even further. The widespread adoption of Java by developers led to a rapid expansion of the number of Java APIs, increasing the scope of tasks that Java could be deployed to tackle. In particular, Java became increasingly deployed as a server programming language providing the centralized services required by enterprises, running on large, powerful back-end computers.

However, the large API set required to support Java in all its tasks posed a problem. One of the strengths of Java is the ability to write a program once and run it anywhere. However, a standard API set is a prerequisite for this as it guarantees the same API call will always be available to the program whatever platform the program runs on. As the API set grew it became impractical for every Java device to support the entire set, particularly with small, memory-constrained devices such as smartphones.

Recognizing that 'one size does not fit all', Sun's solution to this issue was, in 1999, to subdivide Java into editions, each with its own API set. There is now the Java 2 Enterprise Edition (J2EE) for server programming, the Java 2 Standard Edition (J2SE) for desktops and workstations and the Java 2 Micro Edition (J2ME) for embedded consumer devices such as PDAs and phones. Instead of expecting a program written in Java to be able to run anywhere, on any machine, we now have a more limited promise – that a Java program is portable between JVMs of the same edition.

This subdivision of Java into editions for specific categories of device was a practical necessity reflecting the tremendous success of Java. Indeed, it made sense in that, such was the diversity of applications being written in Java, no one was likely to want to run a fully fledged back-end enterprise application on a mobile phone!

Java and mobile phones

Java 2 Micro Edition (J2ME) is targeted at a broad spectrum of consumer devices, potentially running on devices from set-top boxes to PDAs to mobile phones. Within J2ME a specific API set, the Mobile Information Device Profile (MIDP) was created specifically for mobile phones. MIDP runs on a lightweight JVM known as the Connected Limited Device Configuration (CLDC) and proved very popular with mobile phone manufacturers.

MIDP

The Mobile Information Device Profile is a set of Java APIs that is generally implemented on the Connected Limited Device Configuration (CLDC). It provides a basic J2ME application runtime environment targeted at mobile information devices, such as mobile phones and two-way pagers. The MIDP specification addresses issues such as user interface, persistent storage, networking, and the application model.

CLDC

The J2ME Connected Limited Device Configuration serves a horizontal market segment consisting of small, battery-operated, connected consumer devices. This configuration includes classes designed specifically to fit the needs of devices with limited resources.

Prior to the development of MIDP, most mobile phones were closed devices (unlike Symbian OS smartphones) and unable to support the post-sales installation of applications. MIDP changed this, allowing users to download and install additional MIDP applications (known as MIDlets) that ran in a secure, sandboxed environment. Such was the take-up of MIDP that in 2003 some 120 million mobile phones supported it. A year later this figure had risen to 350 million and in June 2005 Sun announced that more than 700 million mobile devices supported Java.

MIDP on early phones provided a secure, but highly restrictive environment (MIDP 1.0) mainly used for games. Java on mobile phones became so popular that very soon pressure was on for a more capable MIDP environment. This led to the MIDP 2.0 specification request and a raft of specification requests for additional APIs (known as optional packages) to perform additional tasks such as sending and receiving SMS messages. Symbian has been an active participant in the JCP experts groups deriving these new J2ME specifications (JSRs). The latest generation of MIDP phones provides a highly capable and secure programming environment, enabling the development of sophisticated applications.

Open programming language (OPL)

OPL is a simple, easy to learn programming language that allows developers to rapidly create powerful applications for Symbian OS smartphones. OPL is an 'interpreted' language, requiring a translation phase before execution and as a result it is made up of two major components. To allow users to run an OPL application, the OPL runtime environment needs to be installed on a Symbian OS smartphone. To develop OPL applications, developers need to obtain the necessary tools and examples in the OPL developer package.

In 2002, Symbian took the decision to open-source the OPL language and related tools to allow its large and enthusiastic developer community to take the project forward in a practical way. The open-source initiative means OPL can be ported by anyone to any new Symbian OS UI platform as it becomes available, and new features and functionality can be added rapidly to the core of OPL itself.

Python

Python, currently available only on Nokia's S60 (it could in future be deployed on any Symbian smartphone), allows developers to execute Python commands and run Python scripts and applications in devices based on this platform. Development starts with the execution of Python commands in an interactive console in a device based on S60 or in an S60 SDK emulator. Scripts can be written on a PC and tested in an S60 SDK emulator before being installed on a device as scripts or applications. Once installed on a device, scripts or applications are executed from the Python environment. Python for S60 is capable of running applications that use native resources of the S60 Platform and Symbian OS. It is a simple and consistent language suited to the development of prototypes or for building proof of concept applications.

.NET

.NET is a competitor to Java, particularly in desktops and server markets, and it shares many similar concepts. Symbian OS does not currently host Microsoft's .NET framework. However, as an illustration of enabling developer innovation across many platforms, it is worth reviewing. Currently, AppForge Crossfire enables Microsoft Visual Studio .NET developers to use their existing skills to create applications for Symbian OS smartphones. Crossfire integrates directly into Visual Studio .NET, so developers can jump right into mobile phone application development using a language, debugging tools and interface they already know. Crossfire is an integral part of the AppForge Enterprise Developer Suite (EDS) which is designed for enterprise organizations and system integrators who wish to use their Microsoft .NET and Visual Studio resources for mobile and wireless application development.

Flash

Macromedia Flash Lite 1.1 is designed specifically for mobile phones that do not have sufficient processing power and memory to support the entire Flash Player 7 feature set available on desktop computers. Flash Lite 1.1 is being licensed in different configurations to address the needs of specific mobile phone manufacturers and network operators. Developers today also have access to the Flash Lite 1.1 content development kit (CDK) covering tips, techniques, and sample code for developing Macromedia Flash content for mobile phones using Macromedia Flash MX Professional 2004.

Java on Symbian OS

Symbian has had a long association with Java technology, recognizing the importance of Java as an application programming language early in the development of Symbian OS. Symbian first commenced work on porting Java to Symbian OS in 1997. After overcoming some considerable hurdles, the first version of Symbian OS to provide support for Java was released in 1999 on Symbian OS v5. The goal behind supporting Java on Symbian OS was to allow application developers to use their existing Java skills, without having to tackle the additional learning curve and complexity of C++.

Java was evolving (and expanding!) fast. It soon became impractical to support the full Java standard on memory-constrained devices such as mobile phones and PDAs. Symbian OS v6 opted to support the PersonalJava specification, Sun's first attempt at a Java runtime environment specifically for PDAs. Java then evolved to 'editions', and in response Symbian migrated to J2ME MIDP as its standard Java environment, opening Symbian OS smartphones to the huge catalog of MIDP games and applications from Symbian OS v7.0s onwards.

However, Symbian provides more than the standard MIDP environment. Symbian has licensed Sun's CLDC VM (known as the Kilo Virtual Machine or KVM) and integrated ARM's VMA Technology Kit (VTK) to provide enhanced performance. Symbian implemented the MIDP API itself to ensure that MIDP is as tightly integrated into Symbian OS as possible.

Through partnership with Sun and active participation in the Java Community Process, Symbian took a big leap forward with its next major release, Symbian OS v7.0s. As well as implementing the expanded MIDP 2.0 specification, Symbian OS also supported Sun's CLDC HotSpot Implementation VM, a highly optimized, high-performance virtual machine. In fact, phones based on Symbian OS v7.0s were the first MIDP 2.0-enabled phones to ship anywhere. With successive releases, Symbian has continued to improve performance and functionality. Symbian OS v8.1 supplemented and enhanced the MIDP 2.0 specification with a rich set of add-on APIs (called J2ME optional packages).

With Symbian OS v9 in development, Symbian embarked on major changes to the operating system with, amongst other things, a new security architecture. Behind the scenes, Symbian has migrated its Java platform to the new architecture, ensuring that from the perspective of Java developers the transition to Symbian OS v9 brings no unexpected surprises.

Mobile Java now and in the future

Java for mobile devices has been a huge success story, with many hundreds of millions of devices shipped and the latest MIDP environments offering a rich optional package set, none richer than that provided by the latest generation of Symbian OS smartphones. Java has proved popular with mobile phone manufacturers and network operators, for whom it proves a relatively standard way of distributing applications and driving revenues.

However, challenges remain and foremost among them is fragmentation. When MIDP first arrived the promise was that a Java application written for one phone (and possibly operating system) would run just as happily on another. This is largely true, particularly for smaller, less ambitious applications, but virtual machines from different vendors often have their own idiosyncrasies which entail that an application written for one device must be tweaked before it will run on a different phone.

Furthermore, fragmentation also refers to the variety of optional Java packages supported by different devices. For example, an application that sends an SMS via the Wireless Messaging API can only run on a phone that supports that API. At present, support for optional packages varies enormously between phones. In an attempt to tackle the issue of fragmentation, a range of standards are being created that will specify which APIs compliant devices must support.

The issue of fragmentation in the mobile Java world is further complicated because the Java 2 Micro Edition supports two virtual machine configurations: CLDC which is a lowest common denominator VM aimed at highly resource-constrained phones and upon which MIDP sits; and CDC which is a larger virtual machine aimed at less constrained devices (such as Symbian OS smartphones) and which supports an API known as Personal Profile.

Technologies such as Sun's Java provide a solution to the problem that any application created in order to provide access to new services needs to be redeveloped for each model of mobile phone.

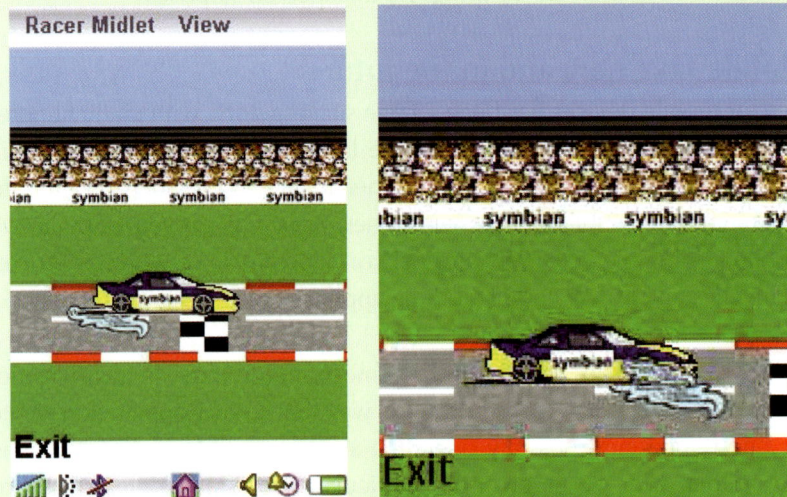

'Write once, run anywhere' – Symbian's powerful Java implementation is best-in-class

In practice, the limitations of MIDP Java environments mean that while they are well-suited to small games, they are often unsuited to providing performance-critical or middleware applications such as media players. But while Java does not have the power or add the same value as native Symbian OS C++ applications, it has a massive installed base – and developer community – worldwide.

CDC and Personal Profile (CDC/PP) addresses some of the limitations of MIDP, but is more demanding in terms of phone resources. CDC/PP is far closer to the Java Standard Edition which is familiar to desktop developers, allowing some J2SE applications to run unaltered on CDC/PP, which is not the case for CLDC/MIDP. In addition to being a less constrained environment it supports certain functionality that CLDC does not (such as the Java Native Interface, JNI).

With different stakeholders (mobile phone manufacturers and network operators) having different directions and plans for Java, fragmentation poses certain challenges for Symbian in its Java strategy. How does Symbian satisfy the requirements of all stakeholders? Rather than trying to second guess the future of Mobile Java, Symbian concentrates on enabling phone manufacturers and partners to provide their own custom solutions rather than trying to anticipate and support every JSR and configuration.

Java remains a hugely important technology to Symbian. Although API fragmentation has diminished the platform neutrality somewhat, all Java editions and configurations have at their heart the Java programming language and common architecture so beloved by Java developers. The increasing sophistication and functionality of Java environments available on Symbian OS smartphones, whether they be CLDC- or CDC-based, provides tremendous opportunities for the deployment of advanced data services, mobile commerce and enterprise Java applications.

Glossary

analog
: The first networks for mobile phones were analog systems that transmitted voice messages as sound waves. Analog phones were less secure than digital mobile phones and suffered more from interference where the signal was weak. Analog systems included AMPS, NMT and ETACS. See Chapter 1.

API
: An application programming interface (API) is any interface that enables one program to use facilities provided by another, whether calling that program, or being called by it. At a higher level, an API is a set of functionality delivered by an operating system, and as such the mix of APIs in a particular system tells you what that system can do. See Chapter 4.

application
: Also known as 'software', an application is a piece of code written and packaged in such a way as to allow the user to 'do' something. Examples include the built-in agenda in Symbian OS, that ships in every smartphone and allows users to manage appointments. Users can customize their smartphones by loading their own applications, which can be bought or (found free) from network operators and online retailers. See Chapter 4.

bandwidth
: Bandwidth is commonly used to refer to the amount of data that can be passed along a communications channel in a given period of time. To be more accurate, both bandwidth and the speed of a connection determine the rate at which a computer or network sends or receives data. As a good measure of performance, Internet 'bandwidth' connections are usually rated in terms of how many bits they pass per second (bit/s).

base station	A base station is a fixed transceiver that acts as the link between a mobile phone and the landline network. Mobile phone networks are composed of an array of base stations that in combination provide coverage of a network's geographic area. Each base station's range of reception is determined by the area it covers and the number of calls that it is likely to process. In remote areas, a base station is likely to forego power for increased area of transmission.
Bluetooth	Bluetooth is an industry standard for wireless short-range communications of data and voice between devices. For instance, it specifies how mobile phones, computers and PDAs interconnect with each other, with computers, and with office or home phones. First-generation Bluetooth wireless technology permitted exchange of data up to a rate of 1 Mbps, even in areas with much electromagnetic disturbance. It transmits and receives via a short-range radio link using a globally available frequency band in a 10 meter radius. See Chapter 4.
C++	An industry-standard object-oriented compiled language, C++ was formally standardized in 1998, but traces its history to the early 1980s, with its heritage in C and Simula. C++ is a general-purpose programming language with a bias towards systems programming. C++ runs on most computers from the most powerful supercomputers to the ubiquitous personal computer. Symbian OS is written in C++. See Chapter 4.
CDMA	Code division multiple access (CDMA) is a digital technology that increases the efficiency of radio spectrum use. In a CDMA system, encoded voice is digitized and then divided into packets. These packets are tagged with 'codes'. All calls are transmitted simultaneously and the packets mix with all of the other packets of traffic in the local CDMA network as they are routed towards their destination. The receiving system only accepts packets with the codes destined for it.
cellular radio	Cellular radio is the technology that has made large-scale mobile telephony possible. Current cellular networks

	reuse the same radio frequencies by assigning them to cells far enough apart to reduce interference. A cell is the geographical area covered by one radio base station transmitting/receiving in the center. The size of each cell is determined by the terrain, transmission power, and forecast number of users. Service coverage of a given area is based on an interlocking network of cells, called a cell system. See Chapter 1.
circuit switching	Circuit switching is a means of creating a connection by setting up a dedicated end-to-end circuit, which remains open for the duration of the communication. Circuit-switched data (CSD) allows data connections to be made over voice networks. The connections are slow compared to GPRS and are charged for duration in a similar manner to voice calls. See Chapter 1.
CLDC	The J2ME Connected Limited Device Configuration (CLDC) serves the market consisting of personal, mobile, connected information devices. This configuration includes some new classes designed specifically to fit the needs of small-footprint devices. See Chapter 11.
content provider	A content provider is a company that provides services to mobile phone users or network operators. These services could be shopping, web surfing, chat rooms, playing games, or accessing data such as music and books through a server. See Chapter 5.
digital	On a digital network, data doesn't need to go through the extra step of being converted to an analog signal. Voice is sampled and coded in a way similar to the way it is recorded on a CD. Digital networks are fast replacing analog ones as they offer improved sound quality and secure transmission and can handle data directly as well as voice. Digital networks include the mobile phone systems GSM, D-AMPS, CDMA, TDMA and UMTS. See Chapter 1.
dual band	Dual-band mobile phones can work on networks that operate on different frequency bands. This is useful if you move between areas covered by different networks. Some networks operate on two bands, for instance GSM1800 in town centers and GSM900 in the rest of the country.

dual mode	Dual-mode mobile phones have more than one air interface and hence can work on more than one network. One example is phones that operate on both digital and analog networks. They are useful if you want the advantages of a digital phone, but regularly visit areas where only an analog service is available.
EDGE	Enhanced data rates for GSM evolution (EDGE) is an enhanced modulation technique designed to increase network capacity and data rates in GSM networks. EDGE should provide data rates up to 384 Kbps and will let operators without a 3G license compete with 3G networks offering similar data services. See Chapter 1.
GPRS	The general packet radio service (GPRS) is a radio technology for GSM networks that adds packet-switching protocols and provides shorter set-up time for ISP connections and the possibility of charging by the amount of data sent rather than connection time. GPRS supports data transmission rates typically up to 20 or 30 Kbps (with a theoretical maximum of 171.2 Kbps), as well as continuous connection to the network. A 2.5G enhancement to GSM, GPRS is a significant step towards 3G, needing a similar business model, and service and network architectures. See Chapter 1.
GSM	The global system for mobile communications (GSM) is the most widely used digital mobile phone system and the de facto wireless telephone standard in Europe. Defined as a pan-European open standard for a digital cellular telephone network to support voice, data, text messaging and cross-border roaming, it is now one of the world's main 2G digital wireless standards. See Chapter 1.
HSCSD	High-speed circuit-switched data (HSCSD) is a technology for GSM which boosts data throughput up to 14.4 Kbps in a single channel and, by aggregating channels, up to 57.6 Kbps. Services can be offered where, for instance, one channel is allocated for the uplink and several are aggregated for the downlink. In most cases HSCSD is available to network operators as a pure software

upgrade. HSCSD started to appear in some networks in 1999, but has been largely replaced with GPRS. See Chapter 1.

i-mode
A packet-based information service for mobile phones, i-mode delivers information services (such as banking and train timetables) and enables exchange of email on mobile phones. Launched in 1999 by NTT DoCoMo, i-mode is very popular in Japan (especially for email and transfer of icons), and it is beginning to make an impact in Europe.

IMEI
The international mobile equipment identifier (IMEI) is a 15-digit number (composed of four parts) that uniquely identifies a mobile phone. The IMEI is embedded in the phone software and also appears on the label located on the back of the phone, usually under the battery. The IMEI is automatically transmitted by the phone when the network asks for it. A network operator might request the IMEI to determine if a device is in disrepair or stolen, or to gather statistics on fraud or faults.

IrDA
The Infrared Data Association (IrDA) is the industry body that specifies infrared protocols. It was originally founded by Hewlett-Packard and others. It comprises a suite of protocols for infrared exchange of data between two devices, up to 1 or 2 meters apart (20 to 30 cm for low-power devices). Infrared devices typically have throughput of up to either 115.2 Kbps or 4 Mbps. IrDA protocols are implemented in Symbian OS smartphones, PDAs, printers and laptop computers.

Java
Java is an industry-standard object-oriented language and virtual machine (VM) invented by Sun Microsystems and formally released in 1996. Java is an ideal language for network applications and applets. Sun's Java specifications include many Java APIs and platforms, including the JavaPhone API, PersonalJava and MIDP platforms, which are included in Symbian OS. See Chapter 11.

kernel
The core of an operating system, a kernel manages the machine's hardware resources (including the processor and the memory) and controls the way any other software

component can access these resources. The kernel runs with a higher privilege than other (user-mode) programs. The power and robustness of the operating system kernel plays a major role in shaping overall system design and reliability. See Chapter 4.

MIDP	The Mobile Information Device Profile is a set of Java APIs, generally implemented on the CLDC. It provides a basic J2ME application runtime environment targeted at mobile information devices, such as mobile phones and two-way pagers. The MIDP specification addresses issues such as user interface, persistent storage, networking, and application model. See Chapter 11.
MMS	Based on the same principles as its evolutionary precursor, SMS, multimedia messaging services (MMS) involve the transmission of images, video clips, sound files and text messages over a wireless network. Designed specifically for 3G (and beyond) networks, MMS allows for the quick delivery of varied, content-rich information to a multimedia-enabled device. See Chapter 5.
multimode	A multimode mobile phone works on multiple radio standards. For this to be possible a phone must have hardware that allows it to process these different signal types. For instance, W-CDMA is designed with GSM compatibility in mind, easing the creation of phones that receive both signal types. This is important as it allows the gradual introduction of WCDMA (3G) networks without forcing customers to give up the wide coverage of GSM (2G) networks.
OS	An operating system (OS) is the minimum set of software needed to manage a device's hardware capability and share it between application programs. Practically, OS is now used to mean all software including kernel, device drivers, communications, graphics, data management, UI framework, system shell application, and utility applications. See Chapter 4.

OTA	Over-the-air (OTA) device management allows an individual or a network operator to make changes to the software setup or configuration of a mobile phone, by 'pushing' a configuration update to the phone via a wireless link. This eliminates the need for docking the phone or going through elaborate synchronization processes and can allow for the simple implementation of firmware upgrades, software distribution, the running of diagnostics and content delivery. See Chapter 5.
packet switching	Packet switching is a technique whereby the information (voice or data) to be sent is broken up into packets, of a few KB each, which are then routed by the network between different destinations based on addressing data within each packet. Use of network resources is optimized, as the resources are needed only during the handling of each packet. This is an ideal model for ad hoc data communication, and works well also for voice, video and other streamed data. Mobile phones with packet-switched communication appear to be 'always connected' to the data network. See Chapter 1.
platform	A platform is a set of technology, which acts as a foundation for real-world applications, or higher-level platforms. Symbian OS includes C++ APIs, a leading Java implementation, an application suite and integration with wireless and other communications protocols as a platform for smartphone creation. Developers target UI platforms based on Symbian OS to develop applications and services. Network operators use Symbian OS smartphones as a platform for deploying applications and services.
push email	The 'always on' nature of the latest smartphones enables your email to be sent directly ('pushed') to your phone as soon as it arrives in the inbox on your PC or company server.
SIM	The subscriber identity module (SIM card) is the smart card inserted inside all GSM phones. It identifies the user account to the network, handles authentication and provides data storage for basic user data and network

	information. It may also contain some applications (known collectively as the SIM Application Toolkit) that run on a compatible phone.
SIP	The session initiation protocol is used in mobile Internet communications – for example, in instant messaging – that provides an agreed method of starting and terminating 'sessions' between connected devices.
smartphone	A smartphone is a mobile phone using an operating system based on industry standards, designed for the requirements of advanced mobile phone communication on 2.5G and 3G networks. This combination of a powerful software platform with mobile telephony brings advanced data services to the mass market, enabling innovation both by device creators and a wider industry of software developers.
SMS	The short message service (SMS) is available on digital mobile phone networks and allows text messages of up to 160 characters to be sent and received via a message center to a mobile phone, or from the Internet using an SMS gateway website. If the phone is powered off or out of range, messages are stored in the network and are delivered at the next opportunity.
TDMA	Time division multiple access (TDMA) is a digital technology that increases the efficiency of radio spectrum use. In a TDMA system, encoded voice is digitized and then placed on a radio-frequency (RF) channel with other calls. TDMA chops the channel into sequential time slices and each user takes turns transmitting and receiving. One call uses the channel at a given moment, but only for a short burst. The channel is then momentarily surrendered to other calls to allow them their 'short burst' of air time.
UI	In the world of smartphones, a user interface (also called a graphical user interface, or GUI) is a customized technology layer that is integrated with Symbian OS to form a complete product. These UIs are developed by 'UI vendors', including Nokia, UIQ Technology and NTT DoCoMo. See Chapter 6.

UIQ	UIQ is a user interface platform for Symbian OS developed and owned by UIQ Technology AB, a wholly owned subsidiary of Symbian. See also S60, FOMA and Series 80 in Chapter 6.
Unicode	Unicode is a 16-bit character encoding scheme allowing characters from Western European, Eastern European, Cyrillic, Greek, Arabic, Hebrew, Chinese, Japanese, Korean, Thai, Urdu, Hindi and all other major world languages, living and dead, to be encoded in a single character set. The Unicode specification also includes standard compression schemes and a wide range of typesetting information required for worldwide locale support. See Chapter 4.
vCalendar	The vCalendar format defines a transport- and platform-independent means of exchanging calendar and schedule data. Any vCalendar-compliant application can send calendaring and scheduling information to any other vCalendar-compliant application. For instance, users with mobile phones running vCalendar-aware applications can schedule meetings automatically over an infrared link or by sending an SMS.
vCard	The vCard format defines an electronic business card. All devices supporting vCard can exchange information such as phone numbers and addresses. For instance, a user with a vCard-aware phonebook application on a handheld computer can easily transfer names and phone numbers to a vCard-aware mobile phone.
VoIP	Voice over Internet Protocol (VoIP, sometimes pronounced 'voyp') is a protocol that enables the transmission of voice traffic over packet-based networks. The Internet Protocol (IP) was originally designed for data networking but its success as a world standard for data networking has led to its adaptation to voice networking.
WAP	The Wireless Application Protocol (WAP) is a set of communication protocol standards that make it possible to access online services from a mobile phone. WAP was conceived by four companies: Ericsson, Motorola, Nokia,

and Unwired Planet. The WAP Forum is an industry
association with over 200 members.

W-CDMA   Wideband CDMA (W-CDMA) is a CDMA protocol
originated by NTT DoCoMo and now adopted for
third-generation use by ETSI in Europe. W-CDMA supports
very high-speed multimedia services such as full-motion
video, Internet access and video conferencing. See
Chapter 1.

Appendix 1

Specifications of Symbian OS Phones

This appendix contains notes on the UI, screen size, and other attributes relevant to application developers of currently available open Symbian OS smartphones. Further technical information and an up-to-date list of phones can be found at: ***www.symbian.com/phones***

Please note that this is a quick guide to Symbian OS smartphones, some of which are not yet commercially available. The information contained within this appendix was correct at the time of going to press. For full, up-to-date information, refer to the manufacturer's website.

Arima U308

OS Version	Symbian OS v7.0
UI	UIQ
Built-in memory available	32 MB
Storage media	Mini SD/MMC
Screen	208×320 pixels
	65,536 colors
Data input methods	Keypad
	Pointing device
Camera	1.3 megapixels resolution
	4x digital zoom
Network Protocol(s)	GSM E900/1800/1900
	HSCSD
	GPRS
Connectivity	Infrared
	Bluetooth
	USB
Browsing	WAP 2.0
	xHTML

BenQ P30

OS Version	Symbian OS v7.0
UI	UIQ 2.1
Built-in memory available	32 MB
Storage media	MMC and SD
Screen	208×320 pixels
	65,536 colors
Data input methods	Keypad
	Pointing device
Camera	0.3 megapixels resolution
Network Protocol(s)	GSM E900/1800/1900
	HSCSD
	GPRS (Class 10, B)
Connectivity	Infrared
	Bluetooth
	USB
Browsing	WAP 2.0
	xHTML

FOMA D701i, manufactured by Mitsubishi

OS Version	Symbian OS v6.1
UI	Custom
Built-in memory available	*
Storage media	miniSD
Screen	240×320 pixels
	65,536 colors
Data input methods	Keypad
Camera	Outer
	1.31 megapixels resolution
	4× digital zoom
	Inner
	0.1 megapixels resolution
Network Protocol(s)	*
Connectivity	*
Browsing	*

FOMA D901i, manufactured by Mitsubishi

OS Version	Symbian OS v6.1
UI	Custom
Built-in memory available	*
Storage media	miniSD
Screen	240×320 pixels
	65,536 colors
Data input methods	Keypad
Camera	*Outer*
	2 megapixels resolution
	12.5× digital zoom
	Inner
	0.1 megapixels resolution
Network Protocol(s)	*
Connectivity	*
Browsing	*

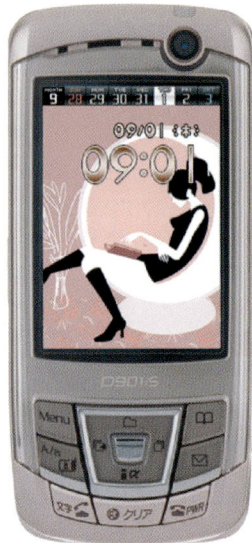

FOMA D901is, manufactured by Mitsubishi

OS Version	Symbian OS v6.1
UI	Custom
Built-in memory available	*
Storage media	miniSD
Screen	240×320 pixels
	262,144 colors
Data input methods	Keypad
Camera	Outer
	2 megapixels resolution
	28× digital zoom
	Inner
	0.3 megapixels resolution
Network Protocol(s)	*
Connectivity	*
Browsing	*

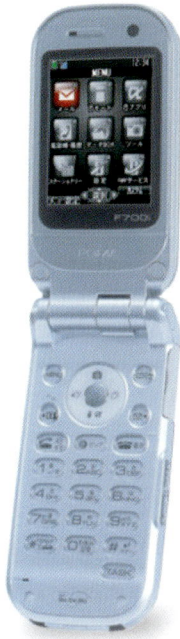

FOMA F700i, manufactured by Fujitsu

OS Version	Symbian OS v6.1
UI	Custom
Built-in memory available	*
Storage media	miniSD
Screen	240×320 pixels
	262,144 colors
Data input methods	Keypad
Camera	Outer
	1.28 megapixels resolution
	16× digital zoom
	Inner
	0.3 megapixels resolution
Network Protocol(s)	*
Connectivity	*
Browsing	*

FOMA F700iS, manufactured by Fujitsu

OS Version	Symbian OS v6.1
UI	Custom
Built-in memory available	*
Storage media	miniSD
Screen	240×320 pixels
	262,144 colors
Data input methods	Keypad
Camera	Outer
	1.28 megapixels resolution
	Inner
	0.3 megapixels resolution
Network Protocol(s)	*
Connectivity	*
Browsing	*

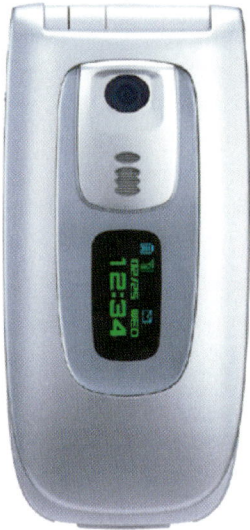

FOMA F900i, manufactured by Fujitsu

OS Version	Symbian OS v6.1
UI	Custom
Built-in memory available	*
Storage media	miniSD
Screen	240×320 pixels
	262,144 colors
Data input methods	Keypad
Camera	1.28 megapixels resolution
Network Protocol(s)	*
Connectivity	*
Browsing	*

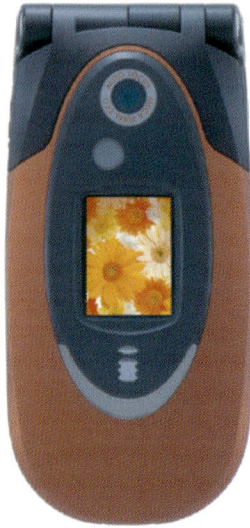

FOMA F900iC, manufactured by Fujitsu

OS Version	Symbian OS v6.1
UI	Custom
Built-in memory available	*
Storage media	miniSD
Screen	240×320 pixels
	262,144 colors
Data input methods	Keypad
Camera	1.28 megapixels resolution
Network Protocol(s)	*
Connectivity	*
Browsing	*

F900iT ブラック

FOMA F900iT, manufactured by Fujitsu

OS Version	Symbian OS v6.1
UI	Custom
Built-in memory available	*
Storage media	miniSD
Screen	240×320 pixels
	262,144 colors
Data input methods	Keypad
Camera	Outer
	1.28 megapixels resolution
	Inner
	0.1 megapixels resolution
Network Protocol(s)	*
Connectivity	*
Browsing	*

FOMA F901iC, manufactured by Fujitsu

OS Version	Symbian OS v6.1
UI	Custom
Built-in memory available	*
Storage media	miniSD
Screen	240×320 pixels
	262,144 colors
Data input methods	Keypad
Camera	Outer
	2.04 megapixels resolution
	Inner
	0.3 megapixels resolution
Network Protocol(s)	*
Connectivity	*
Browsing	*

FOMA F901iS, manufactured by Fujitsu

OS Version	Symbian OS v6.1
UI	Custom
Built-in memory available	*
Storage media	miniSD
Screen	240×320 pixels
	262,144 colors
Data input methods	Keypad
Camera	Outer
	2.04 megapixels resolution
	20× digital zoom
	Inner
	0.3 megapixels resolution
Network Protocol(s)	*
Connectivity	*
Browsing	*

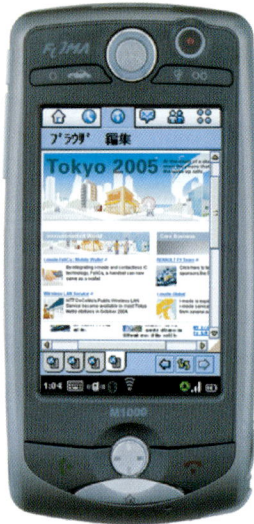

FOMA M1000, manufactured by Motorola

OS Version	Symbian OS v7.0
UI	UIQ 2.1
Built-in memory available	*
Storage media	TransFlash memory and SD adapter
Screen	208×320 pixels
	65,136 colors
Data input methods	Small keypad
	Pointing device
Camera	Outer
	1.31 megapixels resolution
	Inner
	0.3 megapixels resolution
Network Protocol(s)	GSM 900/1800/1900
	GPRS
	3G UMTS (WCDMA 2100)
Connectivity	Bluetooth
	USB
Browsing	*

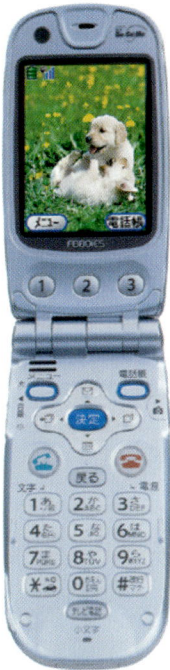

FOMA F880iES (Raku-Raku), manufactured by Fujitsu

OS Version	Symbian OS v6.1
UI	UIQ 2.1
Built-in memory available	*
Storage media	TransFlash memory and SD adapter
Screen	240×320 pixels
	65,136 colors
Data input methods	Keypad
Camera	Outer
	0.3 megapixels resolution
	Inner
	0.1 megapixels resolution
Network Protocol(s)	*
Connectivity	*
Browsing	*

FOMA F881iES (Raku-Raku II), manufactured by Fujitsu

OS Version	Symbian OS v6.1
UI	UIQ 2.1
Built-in memory available	*
Storage media	TransFlash memory and SD adapter
Screen	240×320 pixels
	65,136 colors
Data input methods	Keypad
Camera	Outer
	0.3 megapixels resolution
	Inner
	0.1 megapixels resolution
Network Protocol(s)	*
Connectivity	*
Browsing	*

Motorola A920/A925

OS Version	Symbian OS v7.0
UI	UIQ 1.0
Built-in memory available	8 MB
Storage media	MMC and SD
Screen	208×320 pixels
	65,536 colors
Data input methods	Small number of keys
	Pointing device
Camera	0.3 megapixels resolution
Network Protocol(s)	GSM 900/1800/1900
	HSCSD
	GPRS (Class 4)
	3G
Connectivity	Infrared
	Bluetooth (A920 No/A925 Yes)
	USB
	Serial
Browsing	xHTML

Motorola A1000

OS Version	Symbian OS v7.0
UI	UIQ 2.1
Built-in memory available	24 MB
Storage media	Triflash-R
Screen	208×320 pixels
	65,536 colors
Data input methods	Small number of keys
	Pointing device
Camera	1.2 megapixels resolution
	4× digital zoom
Network Protocol(s)	GSM 900/1800/1900
	WCDMA 2100
	HSCSD
	GPRS (Class 10, B)
	EDGE
	3G
Connectivity	Bluetooth
	USB
Browsing	WAP
	xHTML

Nokia 3230

OS Version	Symbian OS v7.0s
UI	S60 v2
Built-in memory available	6 MB
Storage media	RS-MMC
Screen	176×208 pixels
	65,536 colors
Data input methods	Keypad
Camera	1.3 megapixels resolution
	3× digital zoom
Network Protocol(s)	GSM 900/1800/1900
	HSCSD
	GPRS (Class 10)
	EDGE
Connectivity	Bluetooth
	Infrared
	USB
Browsing	WAP 2.0
	xHTML/HTML

Nokia 3250

OS Version	Symbian OS v9.1
UI/Category	S60
Built-in memory available	10 MB
Storage media	microSD
Screen	176×208 pixels
	262,144 colors
Data input methods	Keypad and rotating music panel
Camera	1.9 megapixels resolution
	4× digital zoom
Network Protocol(s)	GSM 900/1800/1900
	EDGE
	GPRS (Class 10)
	HSCSD
Connectivity	Bluetooth
	USB
Browsing	HTML

Nokia 3600/3650

OS Version		Symbian OS v6.1
UI		S60 v1
Built-in memory available		3.4 MB
Storage media		MMC
Screen		176×208 pixels
		4096/65,536 colors
Data input methods		Keypad
Camera		0.3 megapixels resolution
Network Protocol(s)	*3600*	GSM 850/1900
	3650	GSM 900/1800/1900
		HSCSD
		GPRS (Class 8; B)
Connectivity		Infrared
		Bluetooth
Browsing		WAP 1.2.1
		xHTML

Nokia 3620/3660

OS Version	Symbian OS v6.1
UI	S60 v1
Built-in memory available	4 MB
Storage media	MMC
Screen	176×208 pixels
	4096/65,536 colors
Data input methods	Keypad
Camera	0.3 megapixels resolution
Network Protocol(s) 3620	GSM 850/1900
3660	GSM 900/1800/1900
	HSCSD
	GPRS (Class 8; B)
Connectivity	Infrared
	Bluetooth
Browsing	WAP 1.2.1
	xHTML

Nokia 6260

OS Version	Symbian OS v7.0s
UI	S60 v2
Built-in memory available	3.5 MB
Storage media	MMC
Screen	176×208 pixels
	65,536 colors
Data input methods	Keypad
Camera	0.3 megapixels resolution
	4× digital zoom
Network Protocol(s)	GSM 900/1800/1900
	GSM 850/1800/1900
	HSCSD
	GPRS (Class 6, B)
Connectivity	Infrared
	Bluetooth
	USB
Browsing	HTML
	xHTML
	WAP 2.0

Nokia 6600

OS Version	Symbian OS v7.0s
UI	S60 v2
Built-in memory available	6 MB
Storage media	MMC
Screen	176×208 pixels
	65,536 colors
Data input methods	Keypad
Camera	0.3 megapixels resolution
	2× digital zoom
Network Protocol(s)	GSM 900/1800/1900
	HSCSD
	GPRS (Class 8; B and C)
Connectivity	Infrared
	Bluetooth
Browsing	WAP 2.0
	xHTML

Nokia 6620

OS Version	Symbian OS v7.0s
UI	S60 v2
Built-in memory available	12 MB
Storage media	MMC
Screen	176×220 pixels
	65,536 colors
Data input methods	Keypad
Camera	0.3 megapixels resolution
Network Protocol(s)	GSM 850/1800/1900
	GPRS (Class 8; B)
	HSCSD
	EDGE
Connectivity	Infrared
	Bluetooth
	USB
Browsing	WAP 2.0
	xHTML

Nokia 6630

OS Version	Symbian OS v8.0
UI	S60 v2.6
Built-in memory available	3.5 MB
Storage media	MMC
Screen	176×208 pixels
	65,536 colors
Data input methods	Keypad
Camera	1.2 megapixels resolution
	6× digital zoom
Network Protocol(s)	GSM 900/1800/1900
	WCDMA 2000
	GPRS (Class 10, B)
	EDGE
	3G
Connectivity	Bluetooth
	USB
Browsing	WAP 2.0
	HTML
	xHTML

Nokia 6670

OS Version	Symbian OS v7.0s
UI	S60
Built-in memory available	8 MB
Storage media	RS-MMC
Screen	176×208 pixels
	65,536 colors
Data input methods	Keypad
Camera	1 megapixel resolution
	4× digital zoom
Network Protocol(s)	GSM 850/900/1800/1900
	GPRS (Class 6, B)
	HSCSD
Connectivity	Bluetooth
	USB
Browsing	WAP 2.0
	HTML
	xHTML

Nokia 6680/6681/6682

OS Version	Symbian OS v8.0
UI/Category	S60 v2.6
Built-in memory available	10 MB
Storage media	RS-MMC
Screen	176×208 pixels
	262,144 colors
Data input methods	Keypad
Camera	Front
	1.2 megapixels resolution
	6× digital zoom
	Back
	0.3 megapixels resolution
	2× digital zoom
Network Protocol(s)	GSM 900/1800/1900
	WCDMA 2100
	EDGE
	GPRS (Class 10, B)
Connectivity	Bluetooth
	USB
Browsing	WAP 2.0
	xHTML/HTML

Nokia 7610

OS Version	Symbian OS v7.0s
UI/Category	S60 v2.1
Built-in memory available	8 MB
Storage media	RS-MMC
Screen	176×208 pixels
	65,536 colors
Data input methods	Keypad
Camera	1 megapixel resolution
	4× digital zoom
Network Protocol(s)	GSM 850/900/1800/1900
	GPRS (Class 10; B)
Connectivity	Bluetooth
	USB
Browsing	WAP 2.0
	xHTML

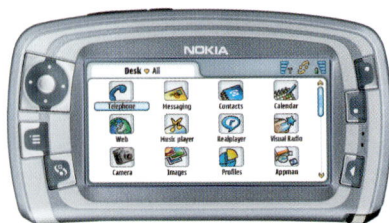

Nokia 7710

OS Version	Symbian OS v7.0s
UI	Series 90
Built-in memory available	80 MB
Storage media	MMC
Screen	640×320 pixels
	65,536 colors
Data input methods	Keypad
	Pointing device
Camera	1 megapixel resolution
	2× digital zoom
Network Protocol(s)	GSM 900/1800/1900
	HSCSD
	GPRS (Class 10)
	EDGE
Connectivity	Bluetooth
	USB
Browsing	HTML
	xHTML

Nokia 9300

OS Version	Symbian OS v7.0s
UI	Series 80
Built-in memory available	80 MB
Storage media	MMC
Screen	Two displays, both 65,536 colors
	main screen: 200×640 pixels
	secondary screen: 128×128 pixels
Data input methods	Keypad
	Full keyboard
	Customizable buttons beside screen
Camera	No
Network Protocol(s)	GSM E900/800/1900
	EDGE
	GPRS (Class 10, B)
	HSCSD
Connectivity	Infrared
	Bluetooth
	USB
Browsing	HTML 4.01
	xHTML

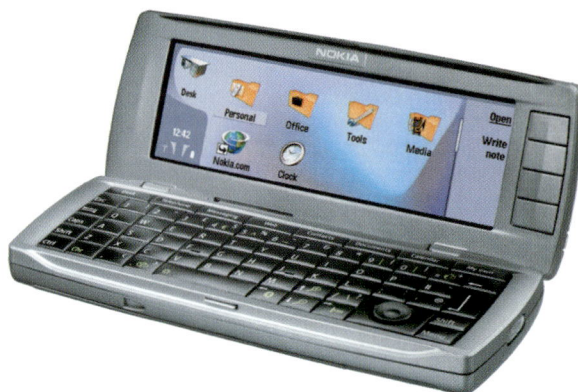

Nokia 9500

OS Version	Symbian OS v7.0s
UI	Series 80
Built-in memory available	80 MB
Storage media	MMC
Screen	Two displays, both 65,536 colors
	main screen: 200×640 pixels
	secondary screen: 128×128 pixels
Data input methods	Keypad
	Full keyboard
	Customizable buttons beside screen
Camera	0.3 megapixels resolution
Network Protocol(s)	GSM 850/900/1800/1900
	HSCSD
	GPRS (Class 10, B)
	EDGE
	WiFi
Connectivity	Infrared
	Bluetooth
	USB
Browsing	HTML 4.01
	xHTML

Nokia E60

OS Version	Symbian OS v9.1
UI/Category	S60 v3
Built-in memory available	30 MB
Storage media	RS-MMC
Screen	352×416 pixels
	16 million colors
Data input methods	Keypad
Camera	No
Network Protocol(s)	GSM 900/1800/1900
	WCDMA 2100
	EDGE
	GPRS (Class 10, B)
Connectivity	Bluetooth
	USB
Browsing	WAP 2.0
	xHTML/HTML

Nokia E61

OS Version	Symbian OS v9.1
UI/Category	S60 v3
Built-in memory available	75 MB
Storage media	miniSD
Screen	240×320 pixels
	16 million colors
Data input methods	Full keyboard
Camera	No
Network Protocol(s)	GSM 850/900/1800/1900
	WCDMA 2100
	EDGE
	GPRS (Class 11, B)
Connectivity	Bluetooth
	USB
Browsing	WAP 2.0
	xHTML/HTML

Nokia E70

OS Version	Symbian OS v9.1
UI/Category	S60 v3
Built-in memory available	75 MB
Storage media	miniSD
Screen	352×416 pixels
	262,144 colors
Data input methods	Keypad
	Full keyboard
Camera	1.9 megapixels resolution
	8× digital zoom
Network Protocol(s)	GSM 900/1800/1900
	WCDMA 2100
	EDGE
	GPRS (Class 10, B)
Connectivity	Bluetooth
	USB
Browsing	WAP 2.0
	xHTML/HTML

Nokia N-Gage

OS Version	Symbian OS v6.1
UI	S60 v1
Built-in memory available	4 MB
Storage media	MMC
Screen	176×208 pixels
	4096 colors
Data input methods	Keypad
Camera	No
Network Protocol(s)	GSM 900/1800/1900
	HSCSD
	GPRS (Class 6, B and C)
Connectivity	Bluetooth
	USB
Browsing	WAP 1.2.1
	xHTML

Nokia N-Gage QD

OS Version	Symbian OS v6.1
UI	S60 v1
Built-in memory available	3.4 MB
Storage media	MMC
Screen	176×208 pixels
	4,096 colors
Data input methods	Keypad
Camera	No
Network Protocol(s)	GSM 850/900/1800/1900
	HSCSD
	GPRS (Class 6, B)
Connectivity	Bluetooth
Browsing	WAP 1.2.1
	xHTML

Nokia N70

OS Version	Symbian OS v8.1a
UI/Category	S60 v2.8
Built-in memory available	31 MB
Storage media	RS-MMC
Screen	176×208 pixels
	262,144 colors
Data input methods	Keypad
Camera	*Front*
	1.9 megapixels resolution
	20× digital zoom
	Back
	0.3 megapixels resolution
	2x digital zoom
Network Protocol(s)	GSM 900/1800/1900
	WCDMA 2100
	EDGE
	GPRS (Class 10, B)
Connectivity	Bluetooth
	USB
Browsing	WAP 2.0
	xHTML/HTML

Nokia N90

OS Version	Symbian OS v8.1a
UI/Category	S60 v2.8
Built-in memory available	30 MB
Storage media	RS-MMC
Screen	Internal
	352×416 pixels
	262,144 colors
	Cover
	128×128 pixels
	65,536 colors
Data input methods	Keypad
Camera	1.9 megapixels resolution
	20× digital zoom
Network Protocol(s)	GSM 900/1800/1900
	WCDMA 2100
	EDGE
	GPRS (Class 10, B)
Connectivity	Bluetooth
	USB
Browsing	WAP 2.0
	xHTML/HTML

Nokia N91

OS Version	Symbian OS v8.1a
UI/Category	S60 v2.8
Built-in memory available	30 MB
	(and)
	4 GB devoted to media storage
Storage media	RS-MMC
Screen	176×208 pixels
	262,144 colors
Data input methods	Keypad
Camera	1.9 megapixels resolution
	20× digital zoom
Network Protocol(s)	GSM 900/1800/1900
	WCDMA 2100
	EDGE
	GPRS (Class 10, B)
Connectivity	Bluetooth
	USB
Browsing	WAP 2.0
	xHTML/HTML

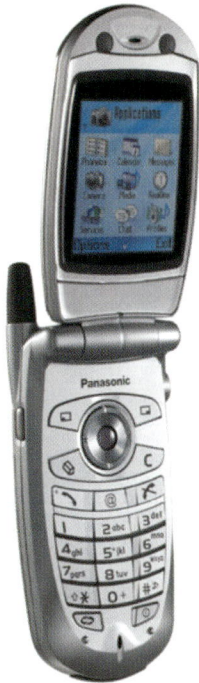

Panasonic X700

OS Version	Symbian OS v7.0s
UI/Category	S60
Built-in memory available	4 MB
Storage media	miniSD
Screen	176×280 pixels
	65,536 colors
Data input methods	Keypad
Camera	0.3 megapixels resolution
Network Protocol(s)	GSM E900/1800/1900
	GPRS (Class 10; B)
Connectivity	Infrared
	Bluetooth
	USB
Browsing	WAP 2.0
	xHTML

Panasonic X800

OS Version	Symbian OS v7.0s
UI/Category	S60 v2.0
Built-in memory available	8 MB
Storage media	miniSD
Screen	176×280 pixels
	65,536 colors
Data input methods	Keypad
Camera	0.3 megapixels resolution
Network Protocol(s)	GSM E900/1800/1900
	GPRS (Class 10)
Connectivity	Infrared
	Bluetooth
	USB
Browsing	WAP 2.0
	xHTML

Samsung SGH-D720

OS Version	Symbian OS v7.0s
UI/Category	S60
Built-in memory available	32 MB
Storage media	MMC Micro
Screen	176×208 pixels
	262,144 colors
Data input methods	Keypad
Camera	1.3 megapixels resolution
	4× digital zoom
Network Protocol(s)	GSM 900/1800/1900
	EDGE
	GPRS (Class 10)
Connectivity	Bluetooth
	USB
Browsing	WAP 2.0
	xHTML/HTML

Samsung SGH-D730

OS Version	Symbian OS v7.0s
UI/Category	S60
Built-in memory available	32 MB
Storage media	MMC Micro
Screen	176×208 pixels
	262,144 colors
Data input methods	Keypad
Camera	1.3 megapixels resolution
	4× digital zoom
Network Protocol(s)	GSM 900/1800/1900
	WCDMA 2100
	EDGE
	GPRS (Class 10, B)
Connectivity	Bluetooth
	USB
Browsing	WAP 2.0
	xHTML/HTML

Sendo X

OS Version	Symbian OS v6.1
UI	S60
Built-in memory available	12 MB
Storage media	MMC and SD
Screen	176×220 pixels
	65,536 colors
Data input methods	Keypad
Camera	0.3 megapixels resolution
Network Protocol(s)	GSM 900/1800/1900
	GPRS (Class 8; B)
Connectivity	Infrared
	Bluetooth
	USB
	Serial
Browsing	WAP 2.0
	xHTML

Siemens SX1

OS Version	Symbian OS v6.1
UI	S60
Built-in memory available	3.5 MB
Storage media	MMC
Screen	176×220 pixels
	65,536 colors
Data input methods	Keypad
Camera	0.3 megapixels resolution
Network Protocol(s)	GSM 900/1800/1900
	HSCSD
	GPRS (Class 10; B)
Connectivity	Infrared
	Bluetooth
	USB
Browsing	WAP 2.0
	xHTML

Sony Ericsson P800

OS Version	Symbian OS v7.0
UI	UIQ 2.0
Built-in memory available	12 MB
Storage media	Sony MS Duo
Screen	208×320 pixels (Flip Open); 208×144 pixels (Flip Closed) 4,096 colors
Data input methods	Flip keypad Pointing device Jog dial
Camera	0.3 megapixels resolution
Network Protocol(s)	GSM 900/1800/1900 HSCSD GPRS (Class 8, B)
Connectivity	Infrared Bluetooth USB support
Browsing	WAP 2.0 xHTML

Sony Ericsson P900

OS Version	Symbian OS v7.0 (+ security updates and MIDP2.0)
UI	UIQ 2.1
Built-in memory available	16 MB
Storage media	Sony MS Duo
Screen	208×320 pixels (Flip Open); 208×208 pixels (Flip Closed) 65,536 colors
Data input methods	Flip keypad Pointing device Jog dial
Camera	0.3 megapixels resolution
Network Protocol(s)	GSM 900/1800/1900 HSCSD GPRS (Class 10; B)
Connectivity	Infrared Bluetooth USB support
Browsing	WAP 2.0 xHTML

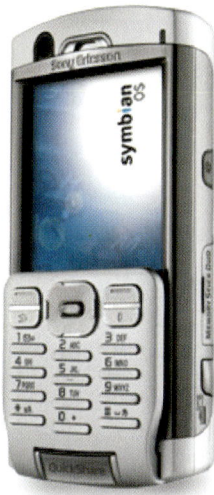

Sony Ericsson P990

OS Version	Symbian OS v9.1
UI	UIQ 3.0
Built-in memory available	80 MB
Storage media	Sony Pro Duo (up to 4 GB)
Screen	240×320 pixels
	262,144 colors
Data input methods	Flip keypad
	Pointing device
	Jog dial
	Full keypad
Camera	2.0 megapixels resolution
Network Protocol(s)	GSM 900/1800/1900
	HSCSD
	GPRS (Class 10; B)
	WCDMA 2100
Connectivity	Infrared
	Bluetooth
	USB support
Browsing	WAP 2.0
	xHTML

Sony Ericsson P910

OS Version	Symbian OS v7.0
UI	UIQ 2.1
Built-in memory available	64 MB
Storage media	Memory Stick Duo Pro
Screen	208×320 pixels 262,000 colors
Data input methods	Flip keypad Thumb keyboard Pointing device Jog dial
Camera	1 megapixel resolution 4x digital zoom
Network Protocol(s)	*P910i* GSM 900/1800/1900 *P910c* GSM 900/1800/1900 *P910a* GSM 850/1800/1900
Connectivity	Bluetooth Infrared USB support
Browsing	WAP 2.0 cHTML

Appendix 2

Ecosystem Resources

Symbian
www.symbian.com

Symbian Media
www.symbian.com/news/media.html

Symbian Press
www.symbian.com/books/index.html

Symbian Licensees
www.symbian.com/about/licensees.html

Symbian Partners
www.symbian.com/partners/partners.asp

Symbian Signed
www.symbiansigned.com/app/page

Symbian Academy
www.symbian.com/developer/academy/index.html

Symbian Developer Network
www.symbian.com/developer

Forum Nokia
www.forum.nokia.com

Sony Ericsson Developer World
http://developer.sonyericsson.com

Index